The Split Brain II

Other books by Aurealia N. Nelson:

Swallowing Jewels

Musings of a Mad Madam

Non traditional Families

Absinthe: Prosaic Bouts of delerium

The Split Brain II

✦

Alternative Research and Voices of Schizophrenia

2nd edition: Revised for 2002

Aurealia N. Nelson

Writer's Showcase
New York Lincoln Shanghai

The Split Brain II
Alternative Research and Voices of Schizophrenia

Writer's Showcase
an imprint of iUniverse, Inc.

For information address:
iUniverse, Inc.
2021 Pine Lake Road, Suite 100
Lincoln, NE 68512
www.iuniverse.com

ISBN: 0-595-25675-9 (pbk)
ISBN: 0-595-65252-2 (cloth)

Printed in the United States of America

To all those who believed in me.

Contents

Part I:

An Analysis of Schizophrenia

Abstract

For individuals struck with the disorder, schizophrenia is a life-shattering event which curtails careers, breaks up families, forfends any possibility of financial stability, leads to severe physiological, psychological and social impairments, and, in many cases (up to 15% of schizophrenics according to some studies) to death through suicide (APA, 1997; Carter and Flesher, 1995; Wyatt, et al., 1996). Schizophrenia's impact reaches beyond just schizophrenics and their immediate families. This is for the families and the search for meaning in the madness.

After the movie "A Beautiful Mind" made it's screen appearance last year—I have been repeatedly asked to make updates to this book and include personal life stories of people that deal with schizophrenia. This update includes new research on schizophrenia on treatment methods and modalities and personal accounts of people who are dealing with schizophrenia. I hope this makes the book a bit richer for the reader.

Introduction

One out of every one hundred persons suffers at some time in his or her life from either Schizophrenia or symptoms of the manic-depressive. This high incidence of a usually debilitating condition has led to excessive experimentation and research to get at the causes of the disease. However, despite the work involved and the progress made in finding factors peculiar to schizophrenics, there is little agreement on the causes of Schizophrenia and little knowledge of the cure, if any. Thus, a person diagnosed as a schizophrenic, treated and released as being cured, has a great chance of returning to treatment or of merely resuming his suffering.

The schizophrenias are a group of psychotic disorders characterized by gross distortions of reality, withdrawal from social interaction, and disorganization and fragmentation of perception, thought and emotion (Tollefson, 1996). Schizophrenia is a comparatively rare disorder—the incidence rate is only about 0.01% and the lifetime prevalence rate across a variety of populations worldwide is typically estimated at about 1% (Larsen and Opjordsmoen, 1996; APA, 1997, p. 6). Yet, despite its relatively low incidence (when compared to other major mental and neurological disorders) schizophrenia exerts a devastating impact on its victims, their families, and society at large. In the U.S., schizophrenia accounts for 2.5% of all total direct health care expenditures (APA, 1997, p. 7). It is estimated that 80% of schizophrenics are chronically unemployed and that schizophrenics account for 10% of the totally and permanently disabled (APA, 1997, p. 7). There are strong links between homelessness and schizophrenia, with studies suggesting that upwards of one-third of all homeless adults in the U.S. suffer from the disorder (Holzman, 1996; Carter and Flesher, 1995).

This report will draw upon the literature to explore the topic of schizophrenia. It will identify the nature of schizophrenia, including its history, etiology, causes, and clinical features, as well as look at genetic, neurophysiological, and environmental factors. It will investigate its distribution in the population and associated demographic characteristics. It will also explore biological, psychological and chemical treatments currently utilized, course, diagnosis, and barriers to successful social reintegration for schizophrenics and methods used to facilitate a return to mainstream society for members of this population.

Definition of Schizophrenia

A common misunderstanding must be clarified before discussing schizophrenia. Schizophrenia is not multiple personality disorder; a disorder with which the split-brain disease is often confused. Take the following two definitions of schizophrenia, noting that within both definitions the distinction must be made that the illness is not multiple personality disorder. Definition One: Schizophrenia is a general term for a group of psychotic illnesses characterized by disturbed thinking, emotional reactions, and behaviors. Schizophrenia means split brain to describe how the thoughts and feelings may not relate to each other in a logical fashion. Often the disorder is described as split personality but this has led to it being confused with multiple personality disorder, a quite distinct condition (Hunt, 1996: 1). Definition Two: Schizophrenia is the term for a group of mental disorders marked by a variety of symptoms. Literally, the term means split brain, but contrary to a common misconception, schizophrenia does not imply a split personality, in the sense of someone acting like two different people. Not until the 20th Century was schizophrenia distinguished from other forms of psychosis (Encarta, 1997: 1).

History of Schizophrenia

Ever since schizophrenia was first identified, scientists have theorized about the cause of the illness. Emil Kraepelin was the first to differentiate the condition of Schizophrenia from other psychiatric conditions. He adopted the name dementis praecox and described the essential conditions of Schizophrenia. Kraepelin believed that the origins of schizophrenia were either a degeneration of the brain or a metabolic disorder causing the body to poison the brain. He also believed the condition to be irreversible, ending in a state of complete and permanent dementia.

Eugen Bleuler coined the term schizophrenia and formed a bridge between Kraepelin and Freud. The word Schizophrenia signifies a split, not in the personality, but between the various psychological functions. Bleuler did not entirely discount the notion of a biological basis, but he emphasized the thinking of the schizophrenic. He was the first to describe the disordered thinking of the schizophrenic, pointing out the impairment of the association of ideas. He believed most of the schizophrenic's symptoms were the result of this impairment of ideas, which he called autistic or dereistic.

Adlof Meyer, like modern scientists, saw the disease as both physical and mental. The physiological and psychological disorders resulted in progressive imbalances. The schizophrenic did not adapt to these imbalances, and this pattern of maladaptation became habitual resulting in disorganizations of thought and behavior.

Freud's influence on all of psychology can also be seen on ideas about schizophrenia. Freudian interpretation thinks of regressive schizophrenic behavior as a retreat to less mature levels of the ego. It interprets the restitutive symptoms as attempts to replace the existing world that the patient has retreated from with such phenomena as hallucinations, delusions, fantasies of world reconstruction, and peculiarities of language.

Carl Jung's interpretation of Schizophrenia is in accord with his theory of the collective unconscious and archetypes. All men have some contact with the collective unconscious as represented in dreams and universal symbols. Modern men have an overlay of personality or persons that is individual. In some persons, the collective unconscious becomes too powerful, and the atavistic tendencies of the unconscious are not brought into adjustment with modern life. The patient's past life and the archetypes that present themselves result in the particular symptoms of each case. Jung's idea of the psychic objectivity of the universal psyche is not unique, but it is uncommon in explanations of Schizophrenia. He connects Schizophrenia with the underlying drive toward self-realization. It is not all individuals who experience those drives, for there are vast portions of humanity who are unconscious and have no problems with that state. However, if an individual is of a "higher" type but for some reason has remained too long in a primitive state, he states:

> Their nature does not in the long run tolerate persistence in what is for them an unnatural stupor. As a result of their narrow conscious outlook and their cramped existence they save energy; bit by bit it accumulates in the unconscious and finally explodes in the form of a more or less acute neurosis.

Harry Stack Sullivan saw Schizophrenia as the result of poor interpersonal relations, especially relations between parents and children. These early relations can cause anxiety and lack of self-esteem. This results in a distortion of the patient's way of living and gets disapproval of this way of living. In other words, he or she lacks "consensual validation." The lack of consensual validation causes a schizophrenic panic.

Silvano Artisti shares this dynamic interpretation of Schizophrenia. However, Aristi formulates the mechanisms by which the patient expresses his conflicts and way of life. An example of this occurs in the area of cognition. Arieti calls the schizophrenic way of thinking paleologic based on E. Von Domarus' principle that whereas a normal person assumes identity on the basis of an identical subject, the schizophrenic, when thinking paleologically, assumes identity on the basis of an identical verb or predicate. An example is given of a patient who thought she was the Virgin Mary because she was a virgin; therefore, she was the Virgin Mary. Being a virgin is the predicate in this case. The patient used this to escape from her own ideas of unworthiness. Arieti has an interesting way to account for the biological theories of the origins of Schizophrenia. He believes that intensely disturbing emotions may bring about the resurgence of obsolete functional and neural patterns.

Changing Stigma of Mental Illness

One of the biggest obstacles to finding a better treatment for schizophrenia, or even a cure, may be the fact that there still remains a high level of stigma in this country associated with mental illness. A lack of health insurance coverage has also been cited as one of the primary reasons why so few schizophrenia patients receive appropriate treatment. Further, the patients themselves may contribute to this situation because schizophrenia is a very difficult disease to manage and to openly confront. "Despite great advances in the medical treatment of schizophrenia during the second half of this century, we remain woefully deficient in our ability to deliver that treatment to patients in need. The stigma associated with mental illness is at the root of this failure and contributes to inadequacies of health insurance coverage for mental illness, lack of information and resources among the families of patients, and the difficulties many patients have in accepting their illnesses," (Dietz, 1998: 2).

Encouraging new attitudes are developing toward Schizophrenia and mental illness. Instead of seeing madness as a total stigma, many are looking to see what they can learn from the insane and others; drug users are experimenting with states of temporary insanity themselves. Hopefully, this will lead us to a new understanding of ourselves, for who can say he or she is not in some measure schizophrenic?

Effect on the Individual, Family, and Society

For individuals struck with the disorder, schizophrenia is a life-shattering event which curtails careers, breaks up families, forfends any possibility of financial stability, and leads to severe physiological, psychological and social impairments. In many cases (up to 15% of schizophrenics according to some studies) it leads to death through suicide (APA, 1997; Carter and Flesher, 1995; Wyatt, et al., 1996). Schizophrenia's impact reaches beyond just schizophrenics and their immediate families. In the U.S., schizophrenia accounts for 2.5% of all total direct health care expenditures (APA, 1997, p. 7). It is estimated that 80% of schizophrenics are chronically unemployed and that schizophrenics account for 10% of the totally and permanently disabled (APA, 1997, p. 7). There are strong links between homelessness and schizophrenia, with studies suggesting that upwards of one-third of all homeless adults in the U.S. suffer from the disorder (Holzman, 1996; Carter and Flesher, 1995).

Occurrence and Cost

Schizophrenia affects men and women equally. However, men begin to suffer from the onset of the disease on average about five years earlier in age than women do. Of the general population, approximately 150 out of 100,000 persons suffer from schizophrenia that makes its occurrence relatively rare (Public 4). However, schizophrenia is a serious catastrophic illness for those that are affected because of its early age of onset and the devastating effects it has on the victims and their families. Despite its rarity, the disease takes up an inordinate amount of resources. "Schizophrenia fills more hospital beds than almost any other illness, and Federal figures reflect the cost of schizophrenia to be from $30 billion to $48 billion in direct medical costs, lost productivity and Social Security pensions" (Public 4).

Theories of Causes

While experts agree on the fundamentally biological basis of schizo-phrenia, researchers have yet to precisely identify the specific genetic links, or to stipulate the exact role of neurotransmitters, or to fully understand and explain the biology-environment interactions produc-ing this mental disorder. Nor is a "cure" for schizophrenia within view. The different perspectives of cause will be discussed below. In many cases, the theories overlap, and schizophrenia is thought to be caused by a variety of factors.

Cause and Etiology

The great controversy in Schizophrenia is the question: is Schizophrenia caused by environmental factors or is it caused by biological factors? Many scientists have now reached the conclusion that it is a combination of both of these factors that produces the schizophrenic.

Despite remarkable advances in psychiatric medicine over the past few decades (e.g., breakthroughs in understanding the biological basis of many mental illnesses, the serotonin hypothesis and the discovery of effective treatments for Major Depression, etc.) the etiology and treatment of what is generally regarded as the most devastating of the major mental disorders—schizophrenia—largely remains a puzzle.

A number of different theories have been proposed to explain the etiology of schizophrenia. Older, exclusively psychological or psychoanalytical models include the double-bind theory and the theory of the "schizophrenic family" (which basically postulates that parents create schizophrenic responses in their offspring as a consequence of fractured family communication patterns and disturbed family relations) (Larsen & Opjordsmoen, 1996; Holzman, 1996). More recently developed, strictly biological models of the etiology of schizophrenia include theories about excessive activity of dopaminergic neurons in the mesolimbic system, cerebral abnormalities (particularly in the frontal and temporal lobes) caused by neurodevelopmental disturbances, and genetic disturbances (Larsen and Opjordsmoen, 1996; APA, 1997).

Over the past two decades, however, what has emerged as the dominant model of schizophrenia etiology has adopted a much more eclectic approach, emphasizing the multiple roles of both biological (e.g., genetic, neurological) and environmental (e.g., family, culture, socioeconomic status, etc.) factors in the etiology of this disorder. The adoption of this eclectic model is largely a pragmatic response to research findings indicating that no single factor (or group of related factor) dominates in the etiology of schizophrenia. The evidence on genetic links in schizophrenia provides an example of the equivocal nature of the research findings.

Brain Chemistry as a Cause

Brain chemistry has been studied as another possible cause, and perhaps as a clue to treating schizophrenia. It is thought that dopamine or neurotransmitters in overabundance may be the possible cause of the electric storms that seize the brain. Technology that is new, like brain scanning, has also shown that there are some structural deformities in the brain of persons with schizophrenia.

Powerful psychoactive drugs are used to treat schizophrenia most commonly, due to the fact that brain chemistry imbalance is considered the primary cause at present, "The drugs that are beneficial in controlling symptoms work on certain chemical messengers. These chemicals, such as dopamine and serotonin, enable brain cells to communicate with each other. Scientists conclude that an imbalance of neurotransmitters is probably at the root of the cause" (Hunt, 1996: 1).

Some of these factors are undoubtedly neuroanatomical and neurobiological. Studies of deficit in intellectual functioning among schizophrenics, associations between risk for schizophrenia and various neurological assaults in the prenatal environment, and the results of brain imaging studies revealing various regional structural brain abnormalities among schizophrenics all provide testimony to the neurological basis of the disease (Tien, et al., 1996; Hanes, et al., 1996; Russell, et al., 1997).

The theory that schizophrenia is brought on by excess activity of the neurotransmitter dopamine is based primarily upon information concerning the mode of action of drugs that are effective in treating schizophrenia (Davison & Neale, 1986). If the biochemical activity of a therapeutically effective drug is understood, or at least hypothesized, the process for the disorder may be guessed at too. Further indirect support for the theory of excess dopamine activity comes from the literature of amphetamine psychosis. Amphetamines can produce a state that closely resembles paranoid schizophrenia, and they can exacerbate the symptomatology of a schizophrenic (Davison & Neale, 1987). It is often argued that excess dopamine activity can be blocked by phenothiazines, given rise to the belief that this may be one of the causal factors in the etiology of schizophrenics with positive symptoms.

Another foundation for the genetic theory is the biochemical changes in the body. The use of hallucinogens such as mescaline and LSD produce in human beings perceptions similar to Schizophrenia, and bulbocapnine can produce a catatonic like state in animals. Also 3, 4-dimethophenylathylamine, a substance similar to mescaline, has been found in the urine of many schizophrenic patients. Abnormal indoles have also been found in schizophrenics' urine, but both of these substances could have dietary origins. Abnormalities of carbohydrate metabolism are believed to be the result of secondary factors too. R. G. Heath has isolated a specific protein factor named taraxein from the serum of his patients. Taraxein is related to the alpha-globulin transporter of copper in blood plasma and is inconclusively reported to have caused psychotic symptoms in volunteers.

However, as is the case with the investigations of genetic factors in schizophrenia, the research on neurological factors in schizophrenia is hampered both by the current limits of medical science and by the heterogeneous and variable character of schizophrenic symptoms which makes it more difficult for researchers to draw clear lines between structural abnormalities and behaviors (Holzman, 1996; Wahlberg, et al., 1997).

Biological Risks

A variety of environmental and biological risk factors have been associated with a greater incidence of schizophrenia. Supporting the hypothesis of genetic links in schizophrenia, the risk of developing the disorder is higher among persons who have relatives with the disorder, particularly one or more first-degree relatives (APA, 1997, p. 6). The prevalence of schizophrenia in first-degree family members is estimated at between 3.5% and 8% (low compared to many other hereditary disorders, but high compared to general population risk) (Holzman, 1996, p. 118).

On balance, there is no doubt that schizophrenia has a large genetic component—family, twin and adoptive studies demonstrates that schizophrenia runs in the biological families of patients even in cases when they are reared apart from those families (Holzman, 1996; Vallada & Kunugi, 1996; Kendler, et al., 1996; Wahlberg, et al., 1997).

There are a number of investigators who consider heredity as an important factor in the origin of Schizophrenia. Among these investigators are H. Luxenburger in Germany, E. Essen-Moller in Sweden, F. J. Kalleman and Jon L. Karlsson in the United States, and Eliot Slater in Great Britain. This notion is very unacceptable to the public and also to those who are trying to cure and rehabilitate schizophrenics, as it is quite fatalistic and the tendency of people who believe in the inheritance factor is to label schizophrenics as lost.

There are a number of different theories about the exact way in which the tendency to inheritance of Schizophrenia is passed on. Jon L. Karlsson did a convincing study in Iceland, an excellent controlled study group because of the stability of the population and the existence of census records that go back at least 150 years and sometimes much longer. These census records record those persons who are mentally ill.

The starting point of Karlsson's theory is the fact that if one combines the statistics for manic-depressive and schizophrenics, the incidence of these conditions occurring is remarkably constant. He justifies this combination by the overlapping occurrence of these two conditions in the same persons at different stages of their lives. The second supporting fact of the genetic theory is the higher incidence of schizophrenics in the same families. To control this for environmental similarities, Karlsson did a study of foster children who were schizophrenic. He traced brothers and sisters of these children who were reared away from home and discovered that the biological siblings had a predictable higher incidence of Schizophrenia than did the foster sisters and brothers reared in the same home. He has also traced mental illness through seven generations of descendents.

However, the genetic link in schizophrenia is neither as dramatic (in terms of rates of family prevalence) nor as easily identified as it is in other hereditary disorders such as Huntington's Chorea and cystic fibrosis (Holzman, 1996). In 1995, researchers located a possible abnormality on gene 6 that may be responsible for the disease. This line of thinking tends to see the disease as genetically inherited, but what, exactly, is being inherited is still unknown. For example, researchers do not know whether it is a faulty enzyme or a genetic malfunction. However, recent discoveries point to its being a genetic defect, "Researchers around the world have confirmed the general location of a gene linked to schizophrenia, the first wide-ranging scientific agreement on the existence of any gene linked to a specific mental illness."

If they're correct-and four separate labs worldwide now agree a gene affecting schizophrenia sits somewhere on chromosome six-researchers may soon be knocking on a genetic doorway that could lead to new treatment for a devastating brain illness that affects one in 100 people" (Talan, 1995: 1).

While this research has provided some evidence for a genetic schizophrenic vulnerability locus on chromosome 8p and/or chromosome 6p21–23, the genetic markers for schizophrenia have yet to be clearly identified and isolated (Kendler, et al., 1996; Vallada & Kunugi, 1996). All of this suggests that factors in addition to genetics play an important role in the etiology of schizophrenia.

Of course, there can be no treatment possible until researchers have discovered much more about the genetic defect and how to alleviate it. However, this pathway of treatment is being investigated because of the wide-ranging belief that schizophrenia is genetically based. One of the facts that makes people think this is so is that there is a higher prevalence of the disease in families that already have someone with schizophrenia in them than there is in the general population. In the general population it is one in one hundred, but it is one in 10 in families already afflicted with the disease for first-degree relatives, (Hunt, 1996). Yet, this new treatment pathway is still a long way from being a reality. The new gene discovery has caused an atmosphere of caution because "In the past, highly publicized markers for a schizophrenia gene on chromosome five were discovered but the chromosome failed to pan out. Even if scientists can isolate and clone a gene, past studies suggest that it takes more than defective genes to trigger mental decline. Research on identical twins suggests that even if both share the same genes, there is only a 50 percent chance that both will have schizophrenia" (Talan, 1995: 3).

Karlsson concluded that Schizophrenia was passed through two separate genes. He reaches this conclusion from observation that when a schizophrenic parent has children, the chances that his offspring will be schizophrenic are only 16%. However, if both parents are schizophrenic, the chances are as high as 40 to 70%. This Karlsson postulates as a gene modified dominant inheritance. He also suggests that one of the two genes responsible for Schizophrenia is also responsible for creative genius, at least in some part.

Other proponents of the genetic theory have different theories of transmission. Kallemann believes in a single recessive gene of limited manifestation. Others assume a dominant gene, and still others a multiple mode of inheritance. However, recent studies of chromosomes that confirmed the heredity nature of some types of mental deficiency did not indicate any specific chromosome alteration in schizophrenics.

Environmental Risks

While concurring that biological factors (both neurological and genetic) play a key—indeed, essential—role in the etiology of schizophrenia, contemporary researchers are also in agreement that environmental factors are in most cases at least partially implicated in the disease. Contemporary researchers tend to emphasize a vulnerability-stress model of schizophrenia, wherein genetic and/or neurological factors create an inherent vulnerability to contracting schizophrenia and stress factors in the external environment serve to "push" the person towards psychological decompensation and schizophrenia (Larsen & Opjordsmoen, 1996; APA, 1997; Wahlberg, 1997). Family, twin, and adoptive studies have for the most part reiterated the importance of the family environment in the production of schizophrenia. These study results demonstrate that highly stressful family environments and highly dysfunctional family communication patterns constitute a very strong environmental push factor in persons already at biological risk for schizophrenia (APA, 1997; Larsen & Opjordsmoen, 1996; Wahlberg, 1997). Other studies have likewise demonstrated that certain types of low-affect family communication patterns can improve outcome prognosis, while high-affect communication patterns worsen outcome prognosis (Lefley, 1997; APA, 1997).

At the same time, these studies have dispelled the myth of the "schizophrenogenic" family—the hypothesis that "a sufficiently dysfunctional rearing family could generate schizophrenic illness in almost anyone" (Wahlberg, et al., 1997, p. 360). In contrast to this hypothesis, the adoptive family studies demonstrate that persons at low or no-biological risk for schizophrenia do **not** develop the disorder even when raised in families rated as highly dysfunctional.

Identified social-environmental risk factors in schizophrenia include lower socioeconomic class, industrialized nation, urban center residence, and single (versus married) status (APA, 1997, p. 7). A number of prenatal and perinatal factors have been associated with an increased risk for developing schizophrenia. These include obstetrical complications, winter birth, Rh incompatibility, low birth weight, maternal malnutrition, and maternal exposure to the influenza virus during the second trimester of pregnancy (Wyatt, et al., 1996).

Psychological Theories

With the schizophrenias and related paranoid syndromes, psychologists argue that we move into a realm of behavioral disorder that represents in many ways the ultimate in psychological breakdown (Meise & Fleischacker, 1996). The symptoms of these disorders include the most extreme to be found in human behavior, and they include virtually all of the pathological processes identified as potentially self-destructive and dangerous to others (Litrell, Herth, & Hinte, 1996).

The psychological approach to schizophrenia views the disease as being related to the environment. There have been many environmental factors associated with contributing to the condition of schizophrenia, if not representing outright causative factors. Being raised by people who have schizophrenia and socio-economic conditions have also been linked to the disease.

Even the way families interact and communicate has been addressed as a possible factor in the evolution of the disease, "Unclear communication within families is one potential condition, although investigators are still uncertain whether this deviant communication is the cause or result of schizophrenia in a given family member. The disorganized family life often associated with poverty has also been implicated in schizophrenia; in addition, poverty may lead mothers to neglect their health, which may in turn affect the health of a fetus or newborn child" (Encarta, 1997: 1).

Sociological Theories

There are many that deny a genetic or biological causation for Schizophrenia and postulate other theories. Thomas J. Scheff postulates a sociological theory. He repudiates the basically Freudian notion that Schizophrenia is something contained within the individual, with the external world merely providing triggers. On the contrary, Scheff believes that insanity is an individual's response to the difficult situations in which he or she is placed. The model for insanity is learned in childhood. When the person deviates from normal behavior, the persons around him act as if he is crazy. Then he adopts the full mode of insanity. Seeking treatment, the individual is more firmly situated in his role. Scheff states, "These considerations suggest that the labeling process is a crucial contingency in most careers of residual deviance."

Don Jackson also points out the ways that society affects an individual's madness. He brings up the example of "wedding psychosis," the malady that affects Muslim girls when they are about to enter marriage. There are numerous other cases when the shape and the incidence of mental disease seems to spring from the culture rather than operate as a biological phenomenon.

Karl Menninger supports a more individual theory that does not fail to consider society. He sees mental illness as "personality dysfunction and living impairment." He continues,

> It sees all patients not as individuals afflicted with certain diseases but as human beings obliged to make awkward and expensive maneuvers to maintain themselves, individuals who have become somewhat isolated from their fellows, harassed by faulty techniques of living, uncomfortable themselves, and often to others. Their reactions are intended to…insure survival even at the cost of suffering and disaster.

Ronald D. Laing has a popular theory that bears some relation to that of Jung. He sees the schizophrenic as searching for transcendence through self-knowledge. The mad person really sees things, but society treats him as an imbecile. Some people choose not to return to ordinary reality. Laing at present is treating people under these theories.

In conclusion, there are many theories but few facts concerning the origins of Schizophrenia. There is a basic disagreement if the disorder is basically psychological, occurring in genetic patterns, or if it is psychological resulting from environment. It is important to answer these questions, for there are many afflicted people being treated without knowledge of the cause, usually on the trial and error method.

Alternatives

Recently, there have been a number of investigations conducted into viruses as a potential causative factor of schizophrenia. This theory is controversial, but some researchers continue to investigate this area because while heredity may play a role in the development of the disease studies have shown that identical twins do not suffer from schizophrenia equally. One objection to this theory is that no research has been able to isolate a probable virus as the cause, but research has shown that drugs used to treat schizophrenia or bipolar (manic-depressive) disorder may inhibit viruses.

Those that believe schizophrenia may be caused by an unknown virus believe these types of drugs may be effective in helping inhibit the effects of the disease, and some research points in that direction. "A recent study published in Schizophrenia Research puts these casual observations on a somewhat firmer footing." Metabolic by-products of the antipsychotic drug clozapine inhibit the growth of HIV in a standard cell-culture system. Champions of the viral causation theory note that other viruses may be similarly affected by antipsychotic medicines. Conceivably, they suggest, clozapine and some other antipsychotic drugs whose mode of action is uncertain might work by suppressing an unknown virus" (Beardsley 1).

Racial Disparities

Interestingly, many studies of this theory have been conducted with members of ethnic and racial minority groups. Of late, the professional literature in the field of psychology has been focused on the question of whether or not African-Americans are at-risk for being misdiagnosed (or overly diagnosed) as schizophrenic (Coleman and Baker, 1994).

Lawson, Hepler, Holladay and Cuffel (1994) studied this issue. They used census data from 1984 and 1990 from 37 Tennessee Department of Mental Health out-and inpatient facilities to determine patterns of diagnosis for African-Americans seen by or treated in such facilities. Referring to the Diagnostic and Statistical Manual of Mental Disorders-III-Revised (DSM-III-R) criteria for diagnosis, they found that the main diagnostic categories of African-Americans were schizo-phrenia, alcohol and drug abuse disorders, and affective disorders. They also found that in both 1990 and 1984, the proportion of Afri-can-Americans committed to state mental health institutions (31 and 30 percent, respectively) was considerably larger than for the general population. They concluded that a tendency to overdiagnose schizo-phrenia among African-Americans was evident.

Worthington (1992) examined factors influencing the diagnosis and treatment of African-American patients in the mental health system. She conducted a literature review of 12 articles published since 1965 on the topic of racial and ethnic factors as they pertain to misdiagnosis and/or tendencies to focus on specific diagnoses when assessing Afri-can-Americans. Specific findings revealed an association between race and hospital diagnosis, higher rates of depression diagnosis in whites and schizophrenia diagnosis (as well as manic depression) in African-Americans. Part of the problem, in her view, is that many of the tests used to identify possible schizophrenia-including the Minnesota Mul-tiphasic Personality Inventory (MMPI) are skewed toward and normed against Anglo-Americans and are not necessarily sensitive to African-Americans and other minorities. Other tests, such as the Allen Cogni-tive Levels Assessment (ACL) and the Functional Needs Assessment

(FNA), do not appear to contain built-in normative biases and are more accurate in identifying schizophrenia and schizoaffective disorder.

Flaskerud and Hu (1988) conducted an extensive study, employing a sample of 24,600 adult white, African-American, Latino and Asian clients of a county mental health system. They found that African-American and Asian clients had a greater proportion of psychotic diagnoses than did whites and Latinos a lesser proportion than whites. Whites and Asians received more diagnoses of major affective disorders than did African-Americans or Latinos, and these two populations were more likely to be diagnosed as schizophrenic than either whites or Asians.

Fabrega, Mezzich, and Ulrich (1988) reported similar results. These researchers examined differences in psychopathology among 5,297 white and 1,376 African-American patients admitted to a large urban psychiatric facility. Results indicated that there was a significant variation in psychopathology associated with ethnicity, despite controlling for gender, age and education. Variation was most pronounced for unipolar depression disorders, but also included schizophrenia, paranoid/other psychoses, anxiety disorders, and dementia. Coleman and Baker (1994) reported that a pilot study with eight African-American male veterans age 51 to 77 years who were patients at a VA mental hospital demonstrated support for the view that misdiagnosis of schizophrenia is of concern in this population. They found that after two investigators separately reviewed the subjects' medical records and conducted psychiatric interviews with the subjects, seven had their diagnoses changed from schizophrenia to an affective disorder.

Concerns regarding this tendency were explored at the 2nd annual Black Task Force Conference held in San Francisco in October of 1984—an indication of how long members of the mental health profession have been concerned with this issue. Fullilove (1986) reported that it was suggested that African-Americans are overdiagnosed as schizophrenic and underdiagnosed with regard to affective disorders because of a fundamental lack of understanding and knowledge of the special pressures impacting upon the African-American family, individual and community.

Further, the situation is also an artifact of the use of test and assessment instruments normed to the white community and not sensitive to the cultural nuances of the African-American community. Ruiz (1985) also explored this particular explanation of the causes of this problem. He found that minority patients treated in American mental health facilities might differ in symptomatology of such illnesses as affective disorders and schizophrenia. Language and cultural differences that impede understanding of minority populations are of some significance in fostering possible misdiagnosis of schizophrenia and other conditions. He argued that it is now necessary to rethink the conceptual model of defining and classifying mental health and mental illness and to take into consideration ethnic differences, cultural characteristics, and social factors.

Jones and Gray (1986) also sought explanations for over- or misdiagnosis of schizophrenia among African-Americans and other ethnic and racial minorities. They found several contributing factors, including the over-reliance on the classic thought disorder symptoms as pathogenic for schizophrenia. With affective disorders, the lack of clearly defined boundaries between normal and abnormal mood and a failure to realize that patients with affective illness can manifest cognitive symptoms. Misdiagnosis of schizophrenia among African-Americans also results from such factors as differences in language and mannerisms, difficulties in relating between African-American patients and white therapists, and the myth that African-Americans rarely suffer from affective disorders. These authors suggested that clinicians and researchers must pay more attention to the effects of cultural differences on diagnosis and baseline behaviors and symptomatology specific to African-Americans (and other minorities as well) must be established.

Other early research in this area also offers insight into the issue. Chu and Sallach (1900) studied the symptomatology of white and black schizophrenics and found significant differences between the two groups. Findings indicated that African-Americans exhibited more frequent symptoms of angry outbursts, poor communication, disorientation, asocial behavior, and auditory and visual hallucinations tan whites. Whites showed more frequent symptoms of unsystematized delusions.

Taken as a whole, these studies—which represent a far more substantial body of research than can be described in a report of this brevity—strongly support the belief that schizophrenia is both misdiagnosed and overdiagnosed among African-Americans.

Characteristics of Schizophrenia

Schizophrenia is not a clearly definable unified disorder. There is no "typical" schizophrenic. The psychopathology is heterogenous and multidimensional (Lindenmayer, et al., 1995). As the American Psychological Association's practice guidelines for schizophrenia caution, "the disorder is noted for great heterogeneity across individuals and variability within individuals over time" (APA, 1997, p. 5). Schizophrenia is most often conceptualized as a syndrome—a "proposed cluster of signs and symptoms whose antecedents are unknown"—involving multiple psychological processes (e.g., perceptions, ideation, feelings, behavior, motivation, attention, cognition, concentration, etc.) (Larsen and Opjordsmoen, 1996, p. 371). The psychological and behavioral characteristics of schizophrenia (e.g., hallucinations, delusions, loose associations, flatness, catatonia, disorganization, paranoia, impaired intention, etc.) are associated with a wide variety of impairments in multiple domains of functioning (e.g., self-care, working, interpersonal relationships, learning, etc.). They are also associated with an increased incidence of general medical illness (e.g., substance abuse, smoking-related disorders such as emphysema, antipsychotic-induced movement disorders, problems related to poor self-care), associated psychological disorders (e.g., depression, dissociative disorders, obsessive-compulsive disorder), and mortality, particularly from suicide (APA, 1997, Holzman, 1996; Larsen and Opjordsmoen, 1996).

Cognitive Deficit Model

Although the specific clinical features of schizophrenia vary widely across individuals and within individuals over time, and are frequently quite diverse, as noted above, clinical descriptions and analysis of schizophrenia have often focused on the structure of cognition and affect in schizophrenia. As summarized by Carter and Flesher (1995):

> A recurrent theme is the description of failure to engage in *active effortful processing*. Schizophrenic patients seem to lack the energy or will to actively organize cognition. Additionally, there is a failure to chunk, to cognitively organize information for later retrieval...Schizophrenic patients, as such, tend to be passive processors of information.... (Carter and Flesher, 1995, p. 211).

Support for this "cognitive deficit" model of schizophrenia comes from empirical studies demonstrating that adults with schizophrenia show impaired performance on tests of general intellectual functioning (Russell, et al., 1997). While it is now fairly well established that schizophrenics demonstrate impaired and/or substandard performance on a variety of measures of intellectual functioning, the long-held view that schizophrenia is a degenerative disease leading to progressive decline in intellectual functioning over the life span has been largely debunked (Russell, et al., 1997; Larsen and Opjordsmoen, 1996; Carter and Flesher, 1995; Smith, et al., 1995). Although schizophrenia is typically a chronic condition, and even though full recovery is extremely uncommon, recent studies have demonstrated that schizophrenia is not, *per se*, a progressive, degenerative disorder, at least in terms of intellectual functioning (Larsen and Opjordsmoen, 1996). As Russell, et al. (1997) found in their study, the intellectual deficits observed in schizophrenics are lifelong, both pre-dating the onset of schizophrenia and failing to show any evidence of worsening over time (p. 635).

Personality Characteristics

In addition to its particular associations with intellectual functioning and certain intellectual deficits, schizophrenia has long been associated with certain personality characteristics, although the exact nature of these associations continue to generate controversy (Smith, et al., 1995; Carter and Flesher, 1995; Larsen and Opjordsmoen, 1996). Some of the traits and behaviors commonly considered characteristic of schizophrenia include social detachment and isolation, idiosyncratic behavior, suspiciousness, an inability to form close relationships, and cognitive and perceptual distortions (Smith, et al, 1995, p. 104).

Symptoms

There are many different symptoms of schizophrenia, but not all of them are found in all patients who suffer from the disease. Usually, the characteristics of the individual that are most affected because of the disease are their thoughts, perceptions, feelings, movements and relationships with others. All of these are generally negatively affected to some degree or another.

Hallucinations—particularly hearing one's thoughts spoken aloud or hearing imaginary voices giving commands or making comments—are the principal perceptual problems. Emotional reactions to a situation appear to observers to be either flat or inappropriate. Disturbances in movement may appear as catatonia, or as apparently purposeless repetitive ones. Relationships with others are usually disturbed, often because the schizophrenic person tends to be withdrawn" (Encarta, 1997: 1).

Historically, the spectrum of symptoms characterizing have been conceptualized as falling into two broad categories: 1) positive (active, florid psychosis) and 2) negative (or deficit) symptoms (APA, 1997; Lindenmayer, et al., 1995; Larsen and Opjordsmoen, 1996). Major "positive" symptoms include delusions and hallucinations, while the major negative symptoms include poverty of speech, flatness of affect, decreased spontaneous movement, anhedonia, and decreased initiation of goal-directed behavior (APA, 1997, p. 5). This positive/negative approach to symptom classification, while useful, has been proven to have a number of limitations. As Lindenmayer (1995) and associates note: "Most schizophrenics present a mixed syndrome; the criteria for what constitutes a positive and negative syndrome are variable; distinguishing primary from secondary negative symptoms can be difficult..." (p. 23).

Coleman (1989) and Zane, Enemoto and Chun (1992) characterize that group of disorders known as the schizophrenias as a group of psychotic disorders characterized by gross distortions of reality, withdrawal from social interaction, and disorganization and fragmentation of perception, thought, and emotion. Schizophrenic disorders occur in all societies, and in the United States it is estimated that about 1 percent of the population suffers from this disorder—an indication that it is far less widespread than either bipolar disorder or depression. The schizophrenias are considered the most serious of all disorders, as well as among the most baffling. These are, ultimately, two different types of disorders; the form may or may not, dependent upon severity, be a psychotic disorder, while the latter always is. There are several types of schizophrenia identified by the APA. The first is undifferentiated type, in which indications of perplexity, confusion, emotional turmoil, delusions of reference, excitement, and dreamlike autism as well as depression and fear. In the paranoid type, symptoms are dominated by absurd, illogical, and changeable delusions, frequently accompanied by vivid hallucinations with a resulting impairment of critical judgment and erratic, unpredictable, and even dangerous behavior. The catatonic type is characterized by alternating periods of extreme withdrawal and extreme excitement. The disorganized or hebephrenic type tends to occur at an earlier age than other schizophrenias and represents a more severe disintegration of personality. The residual type of schizophrenia encompasses mild, schizophrenic symptoms shown by individuals in remission following a schizophrenic episode (Coleman, 1969; Cohen, Allen, Pollin, & Hrebec, 1972).

In the fourth edition of its Diagnostic and Statistical Manual of Mental Disorders (DSM-IV), the American Psychiatric Association added a third category, disorganized, to the previously established positive and negative categories. The disorganized symptoms include disorganized speech, disorganized behavior, and poor attention (APA, 1997, p. 5).

The three phases of schizophrenia

In assessing and treating schizophrenia, clinicians commonly divide the course of schizophrenia into three main phases: 1) acute; 2) stabilization; and 3) stable (APA, 1997, p. 6). The acute phase is one in which the patient exhibits severe psychotic symptoms, particularly those symptoms within the "positive" and "disorganized" categories. During the prodromal period leading to the active acute phase, there is often an acceleration of the negative symptoms. For example, during this prodromal phase, there may be evidence of social withdrawal, loss of interest in school or work, deterioration in self-care habits like hygiene and grooming, and outbursts of anger or bizarre behavior. During the "stabilization" phase, the acute positive and disorganized symptoms decrease in severity, while the "negative" symptoms may manifest in considerable variability. As its name implies, during the "stable phase," the symptoms are relatively stable and mild, when present at all (some patients are asymptomatic during the stable phase). Some patients may manifest other non-schizophrenic psychiatric symptoms during the stable phase (e.g., anxiety, depression, and insomnia). It should be noted that these classifications are made as an aid to assessment and treatment planning for the clinician. In the patient, these phases are often seen to merge into one another without clear boundaries.

Subtypes

In addition to classifying symptoms into types and levels of severity, clinicians follow DSM-IV criteria in grouping the schizophrenic patient into one of four major subtypes, generally defined by the predominant symptoms at the time of the most recent evaluation (hence, the subtypes can change over time). The *paranoid* subtype features a preoccupation with delusions or hallucinations; the *disorganized type* features disorganized speech and behavior, along with flat and/or inappropriate affect; and the *catatonic type* features extreme withdrawal and characteristic motor symptoms. A fourth subtype, *undifferentiated type*, is a nonspecific category used when no other subtype feature predominates (APA, 1997, p. 5). Though it is by no means clear that schizophrenia is a unitary process, psychologists tend to argue that these disorders are characterized primarily by disorganization of thought processes, a lack of coherence between thought and emotion, and an inward orientation away from reality (Meise & Fleischacker, 1996).

Comorbidity

The literature strongly suggests that while depression may play a role in the symptomatic presentation of undifferentiated schizophrenia, it is not the same disorder and is in fact significantly different from schizophrenia. Cognitive impairment in schizophrenia is known to impede psychosocial performance and eventual reintegration into society; additionally, schizophrenics tend to experience worsening of their symptoms under conditions of stress, responding negatively to common environmental and social stressors virtually impossible to avoid in mainstream society (Tollefson, 1996).

Alternative Classification

Conflicting definitions have led Lindenmayer (1995) and others to develop alternative symptom classification schemes. For example, Lindenmayer (1995) has developed a 5-factor model which includes the categories of: 1) negative component (e.g., emotional withdrawal, lack of spontaneity, poor rapport, blunted affect, social avoidance); 2) excitement component (e.g., poor impulse control, hostility, tension); 3) cognitive component (e.g., conceptual disorganization, disorientation, poor attention); 4) positive component (e.g., delusions, unusual thought content, grandiosity, suspiciousness, hallucinations); and 5) depression component (e.g., anxiety, guilt feelings, depression, somatic concerns) (p. 25).

Course of Illness

Schizophrenia has its onset before a person reaches mid-life. The first episode occurs in youth normally, but some people may have one episode and then resume a normal life. Others may have three or four episodes and then return to normal. Still, many others are plagued with the following types of symptoms for the rest of their lives, "'Thought disorders may be observed as a failure to make logical connections or by the development of delusions. The lifetime prevalence of schizophrenia varies in different populations but the results of most studies suggests that a weighted average lifetime prevalence rate for the general population is on the order of 1% (APA, 1997; Larsen & Opjordsmoen, 1996). Epidemiological studies indicate that schizophrenia is fairly evenly distributed throughout the world, although industrialized countries manifest slightly higher prevalence rates than less developed countries (Satorius, et al., 1996). In the U.S., the most recently conducted Epidemiological Catchment Area Study found that the lifetime prevalence rates varied from 0.6% to 1.9% across four U.S. sites (Los Angeles, St. Louis, Baltimore, and New Haven, Connecticut) (APA, 1997, p. 6).

Schizophrenia is for the most part a disorder of adulthood. In most cases, the onset of schizophrenia occurs in late adolescence or early adulthood, with the peak age of onset for men in the early 20s and for women in the late 20s and early 30s (APA, 1997, p. 6; Gur, et al., 1996). Childhood-onset (i.e., onset before age 12) schizophrenia is extremely rare, having about one-fiftieth the treated prevalence of adult-onset schizophrenia (Alaghband-Rad, et al., 1997).

Furthermore, childhood-onset schizophrenia, when it does occur, can be distinguished from adult-onset schizophrenia in a number of ways. Notable is that childhood onset schizophrenia tends to be of a more homogeneous character (less variability in symptoms and presentation than seen in adults). Another noteworthy finding from the research literature is the evidence for a stronger neurobiological basis for early-onset schizophrenia (e.g., greater evidence of cerebral damage, greater intensity of symptoms) (Alaghband-Rad, et al., 1997).

Over the course of a lifetime, schizophrenia affects men and women with equal frequency, although the age of onset for males (early 20s) is typically earlier than for females (late 20s) (APA, 1997; Gur, et al., 1996). Although there are no major gender differences in the lifetime prevalence of schizophrenia, there are significant gender differences in the symptom dimensions of schizophrenia across the life span. Based on their study of 272 schizophrenic patients (divided into four age groups ranging from under 35 years to over 85 years), Gur, et al (1996) found a greater severity of negative symptoms in men (versus schizophrenic women) for all but the 8th decade, when the trend reversed and women were found to have greater severity of negative symptoms (p. 9). These researchers found no gender differences in the severity of positive symptoms across the life span, with the exception previously noted in other studies of the earlier onset of symptoms in males.

Although a small minority of schizophrenics remain symptom-free (or relatively so) following an initial acute episode, for most individuals, schizophrenia constitutes a chronic disorder. The illness runs a variable course, with the majority of persons experiencing exacerbations and remissions, and a smaller number exhibiting chronic, unremitting severe psychosis (Holzman, 1996; APA, 1997; Wyatt, et al., 1996; Carter and Flesher, 1995). Longitudinal studies indicate that both specific and nonspecific symptoms worsen with age, although most patients show a gradual lessening of positive symptoms (e.g., hallucinations, delusions) with aging along with a worsening of negative symptoms (e.g., withdrawal, blunting of affect, etc.) (Gur, et al., 1996).

Prognosis

Schizophrenia is one of the more difficult of all disorders which can confront the social worker or psychiatrist. Garfield and Bergin (1990) have noted that schizophrenics often require either short or long-term institutionalization and care, particularly when they are in controllable states. Until relatively recent times, the prognosis for schizophrenia was generally unfavorable; most patients diagnosed with this disorder were likely to be maintained almost permanently in mental institutions, where the rate of discharge was about 30 percent.

The current outlook has been significantly improved with the introduction of the phenothiazines (major tranquillizing drugs) in the 1950s. Chemotherapy, together with other modern treatment methods, permits the majority of cases to be treated in outpatient clinics (Aberg-Wistedt, Cressell, Lidberg, & Liljenberg, 1995).

Researchers have identified a number of prognostic variables that are useful in predicting long-term outcome in individual cases. In general, better outcomes (i.e., lower frequency of acute episodes, lower intensity of symptoms) are associated with female gender, family history of affective disorder, no family history of schizophrenia, higher IQ, married marital status, low-affect communication patterns in the living environment, good premorbid functioning, fewer prior episodes, paranoid subtype, a greater predominance of positive versus negative symptoms, living in a developing versus developed country, early treatment, and minimal comorbidity (APA, 1997; Gur, et al., 1996; Satorius, et al., 1996; Lefley, 1997).

Treatment

Even though increasingly effective medication treatments for schizo-phrenia have been developed, psychiatric researchers have not yet arrived at a medication protocol which can provide reliable and safe relief of symptoms to all schizophrenics (APA, 1997; Holzman, 1996; Wyatt, Apud, and Potkin, 1996). Coleman (1986) points out that the affective disorders are mood disorders in which extreme and inappro-priate levels of mood—manifested as extreme elation or as deep depres-sion—dominate the clinical picture. By contrast, schizophrenic and paranoid disorders are predominantly disturbances of thought, though they often present some distortion of affect as well. A disorder of the thought processes is not usually a notable feature in affective disorders, however, except perhaps where the disorder reaches extreme intensity. Even here the disturbed thinking often seems in some sense "appropri-ate" to the extremes of motion that the person is experiencing.

Treatment of these disorders is complicated by the very nature of the illness itself; Meise and Fleischacker (1996) have noted that this treatment generally involves the integration of biological, psychosocial, and environmental factors within a comprehensive treatment plan. While the majority of all schizophrenics typically participate in some type of ongoing (even life-long) psychotherapy, some success in using non-pharmaceutical treatments (alone or in combination with drug therapy) and interventions has been observed.

Currently, all available treatment for schizophrenia is inherently pal-liative, versus curative or preventive (APA, 1997; Wyatt, et al., 1996; Larsen & Opjordsmoen, 1996; Mattes, 1997). The scope and intensity of the treatment protocol is geared around the specific phase (acute, stabilization, stable) of the disease within the individual. Regardless of the phase of illness, all treatment plans for schizophrenia encompass the following: 1) establishing and maintaining a therapeutic alliance (essential both to accurate assessment of psychiatric status and to the facilitation of patient treatment compliance); 2) on-going psychiatric assessment and monitoring of the patient's psychiatric status (owing to the episodic, phase-driven nature of the disorder); 3) pharmacologic treatment (used in the treatment of acute episodes, the prevention of future episodes, and the improvement of symptoms between episodes); 4) medical/physical status monitoring and treatment (related both the co-morbid medical conditions and drug side-effect problems) and 5) psycho-social interventions (including family interventions, patient education, vocational counseling, social skills training, and cognitive therapy) (APA, 1997).

There is no known cure for schizophrenia. However, there are three treatment modalities that have been used to help the schizophrenic lead some type of normal lifestyle. We can categorize these modalities into three groups: biological, psychological and chemical.

Psychological Treatments

There are some people who feel that treatment medications are actually more part of the problem than they are part of the cure. These people argue that the drugs are no better help than when people who had schizophrenia were locked up in mental wards or prison cells. They feel this way because the drugs cannot cure the disease, they can only alleviate some of its symptoms, "The drugs in question are pharmacological straight-jackets. They are not curative. In effect they resemble the mechanical restraints-locks, bars, chains-that were in use up to the middle of the nineteenth century" (Whittam Smith, 1997: 1).

Some efforts are developing behavior modification interventions which incorporate self-instructional training have been undertaken. Nevertheless, these researchers have suggested that there is little empirical evidence supporting any particular efficacy for the cognitive-behavioral interventions in the treatment of schizophrenia. Affective disorders such as bipolar affective disorder and depression are far more amenable to amelioration via cognitive behavioral therapy than are any of the schizophrenias. Both of these disorders as well as schizophrenia appear to be amenable to pharmaceutical therapies.

Traditionally, psychotherapy is bypassed in an effort to save costs, since pharmacological treatment is much less expensive. In light of this information, the future approach should be for a combination of the two treatments, and for the Department of Health to insure that health budgets allow for the additional costs of psychotherapy for schizophrenic patients. There is a solution that, while it cannot possibly resolve the age-old mind/body dichotomy, can facilitate progress in handling schizophrenia. The method is to combine medication with therapy. Neither approach has yet been able to provide a cure, but both can alleviate the distressing symptoms of schizophrenia in their different ways. Why not use them together? In fact dual treatment has often been advocated, but rarely put into practice because the cost of psychotherapy is significantly higher than the costs of drugs. It is the sheer quantity of psychotherapeutic work that cannot often be afforded under present health budgets. Typically a psychotherapist may have to work with a single sufferer for four sessions a week over a period of two years and sometimes longer. (Whittam Smith, 1997: 2).

Chemical Treatments

The "first line" pharmacologic treatment for schizophrenia (in both the acute and stabilization phases) involves the use of anti-psychotic medications, which include so-called conventional anti-psychotics (also called "neuroleptics) such as fluphenazine, mesoridazine, haloperidol, and thioridazine; newer "atypical antipsychotics" such as clozapine and resperidone; and other new but as yet unmarketed (not yet approved by the FDA) anti-psychotics such as olanzapine, sertindole, and quetiapine. While there are individual differences in response to anti-psychotic medications, and although these medications differ in both their half-lives (the length of time a drug is active in the body) and their propensity to cause side-effects, in general studies have demonstrated that anti-psychotic medications are quite effective in eliminating and/or significantly reducing the severity of the symptoms of schizophrenia (APA, 1997; Mattes, 1997).

For example, the APA (1997) notes that 60% of schizophrenic patients treated with anti-psychotic medications for 6 weeks improve to the extent that they achieve a complete remission or experience only mild symptoms, while another 32% experience significant partial relief, and just 8% so no improvement or worsening of symptoms (p. 10).

Although anti-psychotic medications are quite effective at alleviating the symptoms of schizophrenia, they all produce a broad range of side-effects which can in many cases create significant medical problems (e.g., anemia, blood disorders, liver problems, kidney problems, neurological problems) and/or cause the patient significant personal and social impairment. Often most troubling from the patient's perspective are the "extrapyramidal side effects" which include parkinsonism, dystonia, and akathisia. These types of side-effects produce a broad range of movement-disorders, including involuntary muscle movements and muscle freezing (often occurring in the facial region, making it more obvious to observers), tremors, and compulsions related to a sense of physical restlessness (APA, 1997; Mattes, 1997).

To treat both the side-effects of anti-psychotic medications and to alleviate comorbid symptoms not addressed by these drugs, clinicians typically utilize a wide range of "adjunct" medications in the treatment of schizophrenia. These include beta-blockers, calcium channel blockers (to reduce movement disorder problems), tranquilizers (to alleviate anxiety and reduce movement disorder problems), anti-depressants (primarily tricyclic antidepressants to alleviate depression), and lithium and the anticonvulsants such as valproate and carbamazapine (to address manic symptoms) (APA, 1997; Wyatt, et al., 1996; Mattes, 1997).

Medication has become the most common method of treating schizophrenia because the prevailing theories over its cause have shifted in the past three decades from environmental causes to brain chemistry. Instead of believing that the diseases is caused by environmental factors, most experts now feel that brain chemistry imbalances and genetics play the greatest role in the development of the disease, "Nowadays giving drugs to schizophrenic patients is often the sole method used to control the illness. The prevailing view is that schizophrenia is organic in nature, and diseases of the brain are probably genetic in origin. The patient is disabled and requires a sheltered environment plus medication. This contrasts with the conventional wisdom of thirty years ago when stressful events in early childhood were believed to he a major factor. In its crudest formulation, it was said that families causes schizophrenia" (Whittam Smith, 1997: 1).

These and other theories continue to be investigated as more technology becomes available that allows us to more accurately explore the human brain and its functioning. The types of drugs that are presently used to help ameliorate the effects of schizophrenia have a tranquilizing effect on the patient. They are sedative in nature and often will cause a decrease in episodes and a lessening of anxiety. In this context, Coleman (1986) notes that the phenothiazines (major tranquilizing drugs) have been useful in treating the schizophrenia and in eliminating the need, in many cases, for long-term institutionalization. However, the rate of readmissions among diagnosed schizophrenics who are on pro-phylactic pharmaceutical regimens is about 45 percent within the first year after release. Overall, about one-third of schizophrenic patients recovers while another third show partial recovery while another third remain largely or totally disabled.

Combination Treatments

While first- and second-line medications constitute a primary treatment modality in all schizophrenia, a wide variety of psycho-social treatment interventions are also commonly used. These interventions, which include family therapy, patient education, social skills training, individual therapy, and vocational counseling among others, aim broadly at helping the schizophrenic patient to adjust to daily living and re-integrate to society following an acute episode and/or during periods of stability.

Littrell, Herth and Hinte (1996) examined the effects of psychosocial treatment and clopazine therapy with a population of 44 patients with refractory schizophrenia and a history of suicide attempts. They found that patients treated with both types of intervention—chemical and non-chemical—tended to progress more rapidly, exhibit a higher level of hope for an eventual reintegration into the social and communal mainstream, and demonstrate a reduction in symptoms as well as decreased suicidality. Patients who received only one of the interventions were less likely to exhibit these attitudinal and behavioral changes.

Studies of treatment with and without chemotherapy also have been identified in the literature. Mosak (1995) offered an analysis of two case studies to demonstrate that therapists do not necessarily need to utilize drugs in treating schizophrenics. His view is that psychologists and psychiatrists tend to become overly dependent upon pharmaceutical treatment when working with this population. Nevertheless, Schwartzberg, Wheelis, and Zarate (1996) have countered by presenting results of several cases in which initial treatment of schizophrenia incorporated the use of clozapine and in which withdrawal of the drug was followed by a period of decomposition and a return to symptomology.

Future Research

Because of the lack of a cure and because of the controversy that surrounds most of the treatment options for schizophrenia, there are new paths of study and research being explored all the time. Once such explorer is a young scientist who won a half-million dollar grant to continue the studies she researched in college about the cause of this disease. Her motivation to study psychology and this disease stem from the fact that her sister is a diagnosed schizophrenic, and she suffered in pain as she watched her beloved sister struggle with this disease. She realized she and her brother had different blood types than her afflicted sister, who was incompatible with their mother's blood type (as they were not).

Thus, Meggin Hollister decided to test her theories while attending the University of Southern California, "Meggin decided to test a hunch that incompatibility between Rh-negative mothers and their Rh-positive fetuses might be a factor in causing schizophrenia. Her hypothesis was that the mother produces antibodies to attack the foreign blood antigens, which, when coupled with a genetic predisposition, may affect the baby's brain development. Since 1968, drugs have been routinely used to stop production of such antibodies" (Rogers & McNeil, 1996: 2).

Limitations of Research

Research on schizophrenia has occurred for more than a century, and intensive efforts have been undertaken for the past three decades. However, most of this research has come to nothing. Yet, one of the biggest obstacles may be that researchers are very often not in contact with the actual sufferers of schizophrenia (as Meggin Hollister was). As such, all too often the experiences and words of the schizophrenic have been ignored as having any value that could add to the discovery process. "Researchers in this field, cut off as they are from actual patients, adamantly refuse to attribute any significance to what sufferers from schizophrenia might say about themselves. Their hallucinations, their delusions, their strange talk, their inexplicable silences, their thought disorders are all dismissed as the meaningless results of convulsive electric brain storms. Attempts to make sense of schizophrenic discourse are seen as a waste of time," (Whittam Smith, 1997: 2).

Rehabilitation

Rehabilitation for schizophrenics is now a multi-faceted intervention approach that incorporates chemotherapy, vocational training, and behavior modification techniques (Aberg-Wistedt, et al, 1995). For these reasons, reintegrations of the schizophrenic into society is at best a difficult task and, at worst an often-impossible one. With more than one million actively schizophrenic patients currently known to live in the United States, and only about 600,000 being treated at any given time in medical or psychological care settings, the question of social reintegration is one of some concern (Schaub, Aridres, Brenner, & Donzel, 1997).

Given that vocational disabilities often are linked to this disorder, a return to productive, functional integration into society (including work and family life) is often tenuous at best. Hodel and Bettina (1997) have identified the conditions associated with favorable outcomes in the treatment of schizophrenia. These include:

1. Reactive rather than process schizophrenia, in which the time from onset of symptoms is 6 or fewer months;

2. Clear-cut precipitating stressors;

3. Good social, work, and heterosexual adjustment prior to schizophrenic episode;

4. Minimal incidence of this and other pathologies in family history;

5. Involvement of depression or other schizophrenic pattern;

6. Good or favorable life situation to return to and adequate aftercare in the community.

Thus, both pre- and post-episode factors are known to impinge directly upon the course of the disorder and the reintegration of the schizophrenic. In general, the opposite of the foregoing conditions (including poor premorbid adjustment, slow onset, a familial history of the disorder, and a lack of an adequate community or family support system) are counter-indicative of a positive course of treatment or return pattern (Hodel & Bettina, 1997).

Similarly, Meise and Fleischacker (1996) have also argued that a combined treatment approach, employing both neuroleptic and antipsychotic drugs, is often beneficial in facilitating a return to work, community and family. Critical variables known to impact upon treatment efficacy include severity and duration of the schizophrenic episode(s), and the nature and extent of vocational disability.

At issue in a return to mainstream life is the question of vocational rehabilitation; for the schizophrenic whose disorder is "under control" because of pharmaceutical treatment, it is vitally important to include a vocational rehabilitation component in treatment protocols. In this context, Lehman (1995) states that most vocational rehabilitation programs designed for use with this population have historically had a positive influence on work-related activities, but most have failed to show substantial and enduring impacts on independent, competitive employment.

This is a critical concern, given that we now live in an era of deinstitutionalization for schizophrenic patients in which many such individuals have been provided with minimal institutional services and then released back into community life. Recent advances in supported employment have suggested that vocational rehabilitation offers greater promise than transitional and sheltered employment approaches. Lehman (1995) suggests that vocational rehabilitation may exert a positive influence on such clinical outcomes as medication compliance, symptom reduction, and relapse. Aberg-Wistedt, et al. (1995) assessed two-year outcomes of 40 patients with schizophrenic disorders who were randomly assigned to either a team-based, intensive care management program or to standard psychiatric services.

The case management model featured increased staff contact time with patients, rehabilitation plans based on patients' expressed needs, and patients' attendance at team meetings where their rehabilitation plan was discussed. Patients in the case management group had significantly fewer emergency visits compared with the two-year period before the study. Their family members reported a significantly reduced burden of care associated with ongoing relationships with psychiatric services over the two-year study period. The size of patients' social networks increased for the case management group and decreased for the control group (Aberg-Wistedt, et al, 1995). These researchers concluded that for a successful return to community life and meaningful work, schizophrenics require a multimodal intervention and treatment approach.

These authors believe that a combination of chemotherapy and cognitive therapy must be understood as offering the greatest degree of hope for a full return to functional participation within the social mainstream. Hodel and Brenner (1997) also support the integration of cognitive and behavioral therapies with some type of pharmaceutical regimen in the treatment of schizophrenics. For a successful return, it is also important to ensure that the schizophrenic will reenter the world and make a close connection with significant others, including family, co-workers, and community-based treatment centers and therapists.

Given that cultural factors often influence the type, symptom content, and even the incidence of schizophrenic disorders, the social setting to which the schizophrenic is returned must be understood as a vital component in successful reintegration.

Conclusion

Schizophrenia is a disorder with a highly individualized presentation, and thus each schizophrenic must be understood and treated as a unique individual. Schizophrenia is the most devastating of all psychiatric illnesses. Its impact upon the relatively tiny proportion of the population affected by the disorder is virtually incalculable and its economic, social, and psychological impact on the immediate family, caregivers, and society as a whole is substantial.

While research over the past two decades has helped to illuminate the etiology of the disorder, clarified some of its clinical features, and led to the development of more effective treatment protocols, schizophrenia today largely remains an unsolved puzzle.

In conclusion, one can readily see that schizophrenia is not, as commonly thought, multiple personality disorder. Nor is it a favorite with defense lawyers as a means of getting clients off the hook for their irresponsible actions. Rather, it is a devastating, personal nightmare whose symptoms and afflictions more resemble a scenario from Dante's Inferno, than the traditional symptoms of the diseases we view in our daily lives. While there have been new pathways of research opened, and while there have been genetic links possibly established to pinpoint the cause of the disease, there is still no known cure.

Instead, we must rely on the traditional modes of treatment such as pharmaceuticals and psychotherapy. Both have been proven to be effective in helping to restore some quality of life to patients afflicted with this torturous disease. However, experts feel there needs to be a combined approach utilized in order to take advantage of creating the most effective treatment option. Despite decades of research and investigation into the causes and a potential cure for schizophrenia, medical science remains unable to provide us with a compelling account of what actually causes this mind-robbing disorder.

It appears that more than one cause may be responsible or that little explored avenues of research (like the viral causation theory) may play a role in the development of the disease. As new technologies become available and as more resources are spent investigating different theories, the future may yet hold the answer to the cause(s) and potential cure for this debilitating disease.

Part II:

African Americans and Schizophrenia: A Dietary Link? A call for more research

Introduction

According to Trierweiler, Neighbors, Munday, Thompson, Binion and Gomez (2000) African Americans are diagnosed with schizophrenia 10 to 40 times more frequently than non-African Americans (typically whites). Because of the increased prevalence of schizophrenia within the African American community, researchers have begun to wonder if there are fundamental differences between African and non-African American patients diagnosed with schizophrenia. The differences may account for the increased risk of African Americans developing schizophrenia and may also provide some insight into how the disease can be managed.

When considering research that deals specifically with schizophrenia and its diagnosis, many researchers have noted correlations between poor diets and schizophrenia (Le Fevre, 2001; McCreadie, Macdonald, Blacklock and Tilak-Singh, 1998; Dohan, Harper, Clark, Rodrigue, and Zigas, 1984). This research gives credence to the idea that a certain diets low in fruits and vegetables can have some intrinsic effect on the development of schizophrenia. When one considers that the dietary formula proposed as a possible cause of schizophrenia closely matches that of the African American dietary make-up, a clearer understanding of why African Americans have a higher susceptibility of developing schizophrenia emerges.

African Americans have notoriously poor dietary habits. Marked with diets high in cholesterol and saturated fat, African Americans represent a segment of the population with the poorest nutritional habits (Basiotis, Lino and Anand, 1998). Additionally, African Americans have higher rates of hypertension, diabetes, obesity, vascular disease, heart attack and stroke than their non-African counterparts (Tucker, 1999). It seems that when it comes to the African American diet, changes could help many individuals overcome serious health problems. If dietary changes can promulgate physical health improvements, is it not plausible to think that these same changes could promulgate mental health changes as well? This paper, scrutinizes the possibility that increased rates of schizophrenia in African American patients may, in part, be attributable to poor nutritional habits. While there is no definitive relationship between African Americans diagnosed with schizophrenia and poor diet, the evidence presented in this paper marks a clear path that warrants further investigation into to the topic.

Schizophrenia

In short, there is no on single causative factor behind the development of schizophrenia; rather, it seems that the development of schizophrenia is a combination of multiple factors including: brain chemistry and malfunction, genetic factors, and dietary disparities (Brown, Birtwistle, Roe and Thompson, 1999).

Brain Structure and Circuitry

Imaging techniques have revealed reduced volume and actual loss of tissue in the brains of people with schizophrenia. Of particular importance are volume losses and abnormal activity in the prefrontal cortex and the temporal lobes. Prefrontal loss affects memory, attention, reasoning, aggression, and meaningful speech, all functions involved in negative symptoms. Loss of volume in the temporal lobe affects the limbic areas (located deep in the brain), which contain the hypothalamus, amygdala, and hippocampus. Activity in this area is related to emotions and memory, and abnormalities are associated with symptoms including delusions and hallucinations, and disordered thinking. Over activity in the middle and particularly in the right front temporal lobes has been associated with auditory hallucinations.

Abnormal Circuitry. Abnormalities in brain structure are also reflected in the disrupted connections between nerve cells that are observed in schizophrenia. Such mis-wiring impairs information processing and coordination of mental functions (Levitt, McCarley, Nestor, Petrescu, Donnino, Hirayasu, Kikinis, Jolesz, and Shenton, 1999; Kwon, McCarley, Hirayasu, Anderson, Fischer, Kikinis, Jolesz, and Shenton, 1999).

Schizophrenia is also associated with an unusual imbalance of neurotransmitters in the brain such as dopamine. Imbalances in the neurotransmitter dopamine are important research targets in schizophrenia because imaging studies have detected over-activity of dopamine in parts of the brain, particularly the left side, where psychotic symptoms occur. Such over activity appears to be due to an increase in specific chemical receptors, particularly those called C1 and D1, which attract and lock dopamine. There also appears to be low activity of dopamine D1 receptors in the prefrontal cortex of the brain where negative symptoms originate (Shenton, Wible, and McCarley, 1997; Wible, Shenton, Fischer, Allard, Kikinis, Jolesz, Iosifescu, and McCarley, 1997).

Genetic Factors

Schizophrenia undoubtedly has a genetic component. The risk for inheriting schizophrenia is 10% in those who have one immediate family member with the disease and about 40% if the disease affects either parents or an identical twin. About 60% of people with schizophrenia have no close relatives with the illness. Schizophrenia with primarily negative symptoms has been particularly associated with a family history and possible genetic components. Genetic factors may be responsible for structural brain abnormalities, including reduced brain size and enlarged ventricles, which have been observed in patients with schizophrenia. Heredity does not explain all cases of the disease; however scientists may be close to pinpointing the genetic locations of schizophrenia, with possible suspects being chromosomes 13, 22, and possibly 6, 8 and 1 (Gottesman and Shields, 1972; Kendler, 1983; Kendler and Diehl, 1993).

Schizophrenia and Diet

While it can be effectively argued that the research that supports brain activity and genetic factors as possible contributors to the onset of schizophrenia is quite persuasive, the reality is that there is also a substantial and formidable body of literature that supports diet as a contributing factor to the onset of the disease. Although a vast majority of the research is not race-specific, the content of the research does indicate that certain types of dietary patterns can be linked to the development of schizophrenia.

In a 15-year follow-up study of 179 patients diagnosed with schizophrenia Brown, et al., (1999) found that of the sample population, 22 percent had died. Because half of the deaths (11 percent) resulted from cardiovascular or respiratory diseases, Brown and his colleagues became interested in discovering how lifestyle (i.e. cigarette smoking, drinking, and poor diet) impacted the mortality rate of schizophrenic patients. In an attempt to accomplish this task Brown and his colleagues contacted the reaming 140 original research participants for personal interviews concerning lifestyle choices. Of the 140 patients, a total of 102 (73 percent) agreed to the interview.

Diet was measured using the DINE, a rate administered questionnaire, which asks subjects about food intake during the previous week. The DINE records the usual consumption of fat and fiber, the dietary components most closely associated with cardiovascular disease. It also records the intake of fruits and vegetables. Diets are then categorized as low, moderate or high in fat and fiber intake and the degree of unsaturation of the cooking and spreading fat used.

The results indicated that subjects generally ate a diet that was higher in fat and lower in fiber than a reference population. No subject ate the recommended five portions of fruit or vegetables per day and the rate of obesity was substantially increased, especially in female participants. While this study does not show a definitive link between diet and schizophrenia, it does show that schizophrenic patients have diets that are substantially different from a control population of non-schizophrenic individuals.

In a similar study, McCreadie, et al., (1998) surveyed 30 patients diagnosed with schizophrenia in Nithsdale, Scotland. The respondents consisted of 17 males and 13 females with a median age 44. According to the researchers the patients consumed significantly less energy, total fiber, retinol, carotene, Vitamin C, Vitamin E, and alcohol than a control group of non-schizophrenic patients. The results of this research showed that among schizophrenic patients certain lifestyle characteristics were prevalent.

According to McCreadie, et al., most patients smoked and were overweight or obese; heir intake of saturated fat was higher than recommended; and antioxidant intake and ratios of serum Vitamin E concentration to cholesterol concentration were low. Additionally, patients, on average, consumed only twelve serving of fruits and vegetables per week instead of the recommended five per day. Once again, although this research does not definitively link diet with the development of schizophrenia it does show that certain dietary habit are closely related to patients that have the disease.

It has been established that patients with schizophrenia have poor diets than their non-schizophrenic counterparts, but what exactly is the link between the onset or prevalence of schizophrenia and diet? This question was first considered by Dohan in 1966. Dohan noted that in certain parts of the world, people appeared to be much freer from metal illnesses than those in the West. Dohan wrote: "The kinds of cereal grain from products customarily eaten may be a factor in the production of psychiatric symptoms" (p. 540). Dohan maintained that wheat- and rye-eating areas of the world had the highest incidence of schizophrenia, with oats and barley areas next, followed by rice-eating areas. In sorghum- and maize-eating areas the incidence of schizophrenia was approximately 25 percent of the wheat areas and in the highlands of New Guinea a practically nil incidence was found. Here no grains were eaten.

Curtis, et al (1984) continued this research when they considered that schizophrenia was quite prevalent in Western and other technologically advanced societies but rare in areas of the world which were less developed such as Papua New Guinea, the Solomon Island and Yap. In attempting to account for the differences, Curtis and his colleagues noted that:

> Grains are a major staple of Western as well as most non-Western populations, including most third-world peoples. However, roots of various types (e.g., sweet potato, taro) were the usual major staple eaten by non-westernized populations of Papua New Guinea, the Solomon Islands, and Yap. And little or no grain was consumed. Where grains (and milk) were rare, overt schizophrenics were rare. In contrast, when these peoples became partially westernized and consumed grains the prevalence of overtly psychotic chronic schizophrenics increased greatly (p. 386–387).

Once a correlation between grains and schizophrenia had been established, researchers began to consider what specific element in grains was causing the breakdown of brain chemistry and thus promulgating the onset of the disease… According to one author writing for *Healthwell*, the dietary protein contributing to the symptoms of schizophrenia is gluten, a protein found in grains, casein and dairy proteins. According to this author, "Schizophrenic patients have been shown to be more likely to have immune-system reactions to these proteins than the general population" ("Schizophrenia," 2000). Further studies have shown that patients diagnosed with schizophrenia given gluten-free diets often improve and have shorter hospital stays for their mental illness.

Supporting these findings, Ross (1999) reports that research from two novel studies linking diet and schizophrenia have found that the inability to break down milk protein may be one of the causative factors behind the onset of schizophrenia and autism. Ross reports that researchers have found that, "When not broken down, the milk protein produces exorphins, morphine-like compounds that are taken up by area of the brain known to be involved in autism and schizophrenia, where they cause cells to dysfunction" ("University of Florida...," 1999). Both research studies demonstrated that autistic and schizophrenic children that were placed on a diet devoid of milk protein became asymptomatic 80 percent of the time.

While previous research had identified gluten as the suspect agent in the cause of schizophrenia, Ross reports that findings from these research studies maintain that while excess amounts of gluten can cause a problem with brain chemistry, the root of the problem lies in the body's inability to properly breakdown the protein. In other words, a malfunctioning enzyme is to blame in the cause of schizophrenia.

As research into the links between diet and schizophrenia continue to proliferate, so do the possible causative factors. As reported by the Omega-3 Mental Health Research Group from the University of Sheffield (2001) there is now increasing evidence to support the idea that there is a very strong relationship between schizophrenia and a diet containing polyunsaturated fatty acids (PUFA) from fish and vegetable sources compared with PUFAs from animals and birds. These researchers report that in studies conducted with patients diagnosed with schizophrenia, patients whose diets were modified to include PUFAs from fish and vegetable sources improved over those who has no dietary modifications whatsoever.

Additionally, the Omega-3 Mental Health Research Group reports that in a study that they conducted, they found a significant correlation between omega-3 fatty acid intake and the severity of schizophrenic symptoms in patients. By offering a supplement of the omega-3 fatty acid, found most commonly in fish and vegetable oils, the Omega-3 Research Team found that schizophrenic patients garnered significant improvements in symptoms. Although the exact biochemical link between omega-3 fatty acid and the development of schizophrenia is not fully understood, researchers maintain that patients who have diets that are low in fruits and vegetables and high in saturated fats from meat and bird products are at higher risk for the onset of the disease.

This research has been supported by Le Fevre (2001), who notes that a growing body of research indicates that fatty acid metabolism may be abnormal in patients with schizophrenia. According to Le Fevre, in schizophrenic patients, erythrocyte cell membranes have been shown to contain low levels of PUFAs due to increases in the breakdown of phospholipase-A2. What this means is that:

> Patients with schizophrenia living in a community tend to chose a diet with high levels of saturated fat and low levels of antioxidants. Such a diet has been clearly linked with weight gain and cardiovascular disease. The possibility exists that dietary manipulation, including supplements may both improve the symptoms of schizophrenia as well as decreasing the risk of vascular disease (p. 11).

Le Fevre notes that a study of 20 schizophrenic patients given essential fatty acid supplements, resulted in the improvement of symptoms for all patients.

African Americans and Diet

The African American diet is characteristically categorized as high in saturated fats from meat and butter and low in vegetables and fruits (Airhihenbuwa, Kumanyika, Agurs, Lowe, Saunders and Morssink, 1996; Basiotis, et al., 1998; Luke, Cooper, Prewitt, Adebowale, Adeyemo and Forrester, 2001). In fact according to Basiotis, et al., (1998) African Americans have the lowest Healthy Eating Index (HEI) when compared to other ethnic populations in the United States.

The Health Eating Index contains 10 components for measuring the aspects of a healthy diet. Among the criteria are included:

A measurement that determines how well an individual's diet conforms to the USDA's Food Guide Pyramid.

A measurement of total fat consumption as a percentage of total calorie intake.

A measurement of total saturated fat consumption as a percentage of calorie intake.

While the HEI take other measurements into consideration, the factors listed above are most pertinent to the classification of the African American diet as being a causative factor in development of schizophrenia.

According to the results of the HEI. The mean score for African Americans was 59, compared with 64 for Whites and 65 for other racial groups (which included Asian/Pacific Islander, American Indians and Alaskan Natives). Appendix 1 provides a comparative breakdown of the HEI, which shows how African American scored in relation to other races in each of the components used to determine the HEI. Careful examination of the data reveals that while African Americans did not have the highest level of saturated fats or total fat in their diet, they do have lowest level of fruit and vegetable content(3.5 and 5.7, respectively) and the lowest degree of variety (6.7). According to Basiotis and his colleagues, the reason for such disparities in the African

American diet can make individuals of this race more susceptible to having a less-that-ideal diet.

Considering the disparities in the African American diet, one begins to wonder what the root causes of such poor eating habit are. Several research studies have been undertaken in an attempt to address this issue and all have come to one conclusion: The development of the African American diet is due in large part to the nutritional habits gleaned from African American slaves (Axelson, 1986; Airhihenbuwa, 1986; Kittler and Sucher, 1989; Luke, et al., 2001). In fact as reported by one author, Lizzie McCloud, an ex-slave remembered that she, "ate out of a trough with a wooden spoon. Mush and Milk…Didn't know what meat was. Never got a taste of eggs" ("African Americans," 2001).

The fact that African American diet has largely been influenced by slavery, is a fact that is also addressed by Luke, et al., (2001). According to Luke and her colleagues, although African Americans do retain some of their ancestral dietary habits, Westernization of diet for the African American has meant a diet that relies on saturated fats from meat as the primary energy source for African Americans. According to Luke's analysis, the African American diet represents the synthesis of a too many carbohydrates coupled with an overwhelming amount of saturated fat.

Putting it all together: African Americans, Schizophrenia and Diet

It seems that when it comes to the African American diet, there are a myriad of possibilities that can be causing a higher rate of schizophrenia. Slave diets, which consisted mainly of grains and milk, still persist within the community, even today. As noted earlier, the body's inability to break down the protein, gluten may be one of the underpinning factors behind the development of schizophrenia ("Schizophrenia," 2000; Ross, 1999). Because of this it is quite plausible to assume that one of the reasons that African Americans experience a higher rate of schizophrenia is because their diets contain higher levels of grains and milk products that simply cannot be correctly broken down by the body.

Further, many African American diets have substantially large amounts of saturated fats incorporated into them coupled with low intakes of fruits and vegetables (Airhihenbuwa, Kumanyika, Agurs, Lowe, Saunders and Morssink, 1996; Basiotis, et al., 1998; Luke, Cooper, Prewitt, Adebowale, Adeyemo and Forrester, 2001). Several recent research studies have shown that this type of diet may also promulgate the development of schizophrenia (Omega-3 Mental Health Research Group, 2001; Le Fevre, 2001).

In many respects, the African American diet is a double-edged sword; for the part of the population the relies on grains and milk as the main source of energy, there is research to support that this type of diet may cause schizophrenia; for the African American population that relies on saturated fat as the main source of dietary energy, there is evidence to support the development of schizophrenia. It seems that at every turn, the Africa American diet raises red flags that should signal to doctors and researchers that there may be a definitive link between African Americans diagnosed with schizophrenia and diet.

Analyzing dietary patterns and the role they play in the development of schizophrenia is no different than considering how dietary patterns affect the development of heart disease, hypertension or diabetes. Because African American experience such disproportional higher rates of schizophrenic diagnosis, a closer look into dietary patterns and how they influence the development of the disease is warranted. In this case, the evidence is there, it simply needs to be brought together in a research study that can conclusively prove the link.

Appendix A:

Health Eating Index: Overall and competent means scores for people by race, 1994–96 [*]

	African Americans	*White*	*Other*
Overall	59	64	65
Components			
Grains	6.1	6.7	6.9
Vegetables	5.7	6.3	3.2
Fruits	3.5	3.9	4.4
Milk	4.2	5.7	4.9
Meat	7.0	6.4	6.8
Total Fat	6.2	6.8	7.4
Saturated Fat	6.0	6.4	7.0
Cholesterol	7.4	8.0	7.3
Sodium	6.6	6.3	6.3
Variety	6.7	7.8	7.9

[*]   Data courtesy of Basiotis, et al., (1998).

Part III:

Celiac Disease and Schizophrenia?

Celiac Disease:
Etiology, Characteristics, Prognosis

Celiac disease is a chronic digestive disorder that prevents proper absorption of certain types of grains. Celiac disease is often referred to in lay terms as gluten intolerance, and it is known variously in the medical literature as gluten sensitive enteropathy, gluten intolerant enteropathy, nontropical sprue, celiac sprue, or coeliac. Celiac is often concomitant with or related to a number of other conditions, such as scleroderma, Sjogren's syndrome, Type I insulin dependent diabetes mellitus, Graves' disease, chronic active hepatitis, Addison's disease, systemic lupus erythematosus, and myasthenia gravis.

Although there has been a considerable amount of debate about the etiology of celiac disease, the current data suggests that the large majority of cases are genetic in origin. There is strong statistical linkage between family members with the disease, with approximately ten percent of patients diagnosed with celiac disease reporting close relatives who also suffer from the condition (Maki and Collin 1756). Celiac disease is considered a common condition, with a recent random test of donated blood samples suggesting that as many as 1 in 200 Americans may have the condition. There seems to be a strong association between certain ethnic heritages and celiac disease, as suggested by its increased incidence among certain ethnic populations, particularly people of Irish descent.

The primary characteristic of celiac disease is damage to the small intestine that occurs as a result of a chronic reaction to a component of glutens known as gliadin, particularly those associated with wheat and wheat-based food products (Hadjivassiliou, Grunewald, and Davies-Jones 1710). The main consequence of this intolerant reaction to gliadins and glutens is mucosal damage to the small intestine, destroying the villi and promoting the growth of crypt cells. Both of these processes interfere with the proper absorption of nutrients, which can result in a whole array of conditions stemming from malnutrition or deficiencies of vitamins or minerals (Feighery 237).

The symptomology associated with celiac disease is notoriously divergent, since the condition can have its onset at any point within the human life span. Even when the condition is present, the patient may not be experiencing any tangible signs or symptoms, so diagnosis is often difficult. Additionally, patients with celiac disease do not all present with similar symptoms, further complicating correct diagnosis and timely treatment. The most commonly reported symptom among adult and children with celiac disease is general irritability and unease. Other symptoms range widely, but can include one or more of the following: unexplained weight loss, recurring diarrhea, recurring steatorrhea, pale, malodorous stool, changes in behavior, pain in joints and bones, excessive flatulence, amenorrhea, muscle cramps, small stature or delays in growth, generalized fatigue and malaise, seizure activity, numbness, tingling, problems with teeth, gums, and oral mucosa, and rashes on skin (Pruessner 1027).

As previously mentioned, lack of consistent symptomology renders successful and timely diagnosis of celiac disease a challenge for health care practitioners. However, in light of the serious potential complications that can occur as a result of untreated celiac disease, it is important that physicians and other health care workers remain educated and abreast in developments in diagnosis (Fasano 769).

Although gluten intolerance is often likened to food allergies, this comparison belittles the serious complications associated with untreated celiac disease. Without proper treatment, celiac disease is fatal, and even in cases with delayed diagnosis, serious damage has often occurred, to the extent that the patient's normal functioning has been significantly impaired.

As previously stated, the most severe complications associated with celiac disease are related to lack of proper absorption of nutritional ingredients and the damage to the mucosa of the small intestine. However, the results of these problems can have a variety of outcomes.

Osteoporosis is an example of the type of complication of celiac disease that is related to improper absorption of nutrients, in this case, calcium. Because patients with celiac disease cannot properly absorb calcium, despite the level of their calcium intake, they tend to develop osteoporosis and the symptoms associated with that condition, such as brittle, fragile bones, and decreased bone density (Catassi and Ratsch 202).

Another common complication of celiac disease is growth delays and short stature. This is particularly common when children with celiac disease are not properly diagnosed and treated. The lack of normal growth is usually a result of malnutrition and improper absorption of key vitamins and minerals (Walling 502). Similarly, seizure activity is common in celiac disease patients, usually associated with a chronic lack of folic acid. Long-term folic acid deficiencies can tend to cause minute deposits of calcium, or calcifications, on the brain, and these growths are thought to be responsible for causing the seizures that celiac disease patients often experience.

Among female patients with celiac disease, miscarriage of pregnancy and bearing infants with severe birth defects are extremely common. In fact, many women are diagnosed with celiac disease as a result of the barrage of testing that is often undertaken in the aftermath of repeated miscarriages. The high prevalence of miscarriages and birth defects in the pregnancies of female celiac disease patients can be attributed to the inability of these women of absorbing the degree of nutrients needed to sustain a normal, healthy pregnancy to full term. Although this link has not yet been fully explored in research, recent studies have suggested that the lack of sufficient folic acid may play a large role in the reproductive difficulties associated with female celiac disease patients.

Probably the most serious complications associated with the population of patients diagnosed with celiac disease is that of dramatically increased risk for developing certain malignancies in the digestive system. The most common instances of this complication include the much-increased risk of both lymphoma and adenocarcinoma among celiac disease patients.

Just as the symptoms and time of onset associated with celiac disease vary widely from patient to patient, the prognosis of the disease has just as broad a range. Depending on the severity of the disease at onset, prognosis can vary from minimal to grave, with the most serious cases occurring in those patients who are diagnosed with celiac disease retroactively following a primary diagnosis of a gastrointestinal malignancy. The relatively recent introduction of the gluten-free diet as a treatment for celiac disease has substantially decreased the rate of morbidity associated with the diagnosis, but it has by no means eradicated the possibility of death as a result of celiac disease.

At this time, the only treatment that is prescribed for patients with celiac disease is that of dietary modification. This takes the form of both dietary restrictions, in the elimination of the grains that aggravate the condition, and dietary supplements, usually in the form of the vitamins and minerals that have been improperly absorbed as a result of the celiac disease.

Because the only successful treatment for celiac disease is complete abstinence from the ingestion of foodstuffs containing gluten, patients are often initially optimistic about the relative ease of maintaining their gastrointestinal health. However, few patients have a full understanding of the extent of the vigilance that is necessary to exclude all glutens from their diet.

Although removing products containing gluten from one's diet would appear to be a fairly simply task, it usually proves to be more difficult that patients initially suppose it to be, because glutens are used in a wide variety of commercially processed food products, even many of those that one would not normally associate with grains.

In addition, the trade names of products containing glutens or gliadin vary widely, so that it is often difficult for patients to identify the presence of potentially harmful ingredients simply by perusing the product's listed components (Guest 46). However, in recent years, product labeling has improved in many aspects, and the clear labeling of gluten-free products has increased exponentially, facilitating the making of health food choices for celiac patients.

Although an informed celiac patient can live symptom-free with strict adherence to a gluten-free dietary regimen, this prospect often proves daunting for patients, particularly those who have only recently been diagnosed with celiac disease. Fortunately, there are a number of organizations that seek to serve as support systems and informational resources to celiac patients and their families. A substantial number of these organizations have developed advanced Internet sites that provide helpful and accurate information to celiac disease patients, or celiacs, as they are referred to by many patient support and advocacy groups. In addition, these web sites provide shopping information, connecting patients with manufacturers who cater to the gluten-free niche market.

Some of the most comprehensive and helpful of these online resources include **www.celiac.org**, the Internet home of the Celiac Disease Foundation, and **www.gluten.net**, the web site maintained by the Gluten Intolerance Group of North America.

Part IV:

Cognitive Behavior Therapy for Schizophrenia: A Research Proposal

Abstract

A research study is proposed to assess the appropriateness of cognitive behavioral therapy for schizophrenia. The purpose of the proposed study will be to investigate the effectiveness of cognitive behavioral therapy in the treatment of adult male patients.

Schizophrenia has been studied exhaustively, and many research findings either are inconsistent or conflict with other findings. Schizophrenia traditionally has been The treated through a combination of drug therapy and rehabilitation. The level of emphasis between drug therapy and rehabilitation in the treatment of schizophrenia largely has been determined both by the specific disturbance characteristics and the individual patient. Relatively recent research, however, has indicated that cognitive behavioral therapy may produce significant benefits for schizophrenic patients. The proposed experimental model will be applied to a population of adult males (aged 30–40 years old) in a residential care environment who have been diagnosed as schizophrenic. The proposed experimental model will incorporate the concepts of recognition of existing state and the defining of a desired end state. Within this context, the Outcome measure that will be used to evaluate the experimental model are (1) change in the level of interpersonal skills, and changes in the symptomatic characteristics of schizophrenia as defined by DSM-IV.

COGNITIVE BEHAVIOR THERAPY FOR SCHIZOPHRENIA: A
RESEARCH PROPOSAL

Introduction

Schizophrenia has been studied exhaustively, and many research findings either are inconsistent or conflict with other findings (Johnstone, 1993, p. 536). Schizophrenia traditionally has been The treated through a combination of drug therapy and rehabilitation (Kaplan & Sadock, 1991, p. 1206). The level of emphasis between drug therapy and rehabilitation in the treatment of schizophrenia largely has been determined both by the specific disturbance characteristics and the individual patient. Relatively recent research, however, has indicated that cognitive behavioral therapy may produce significant benefits for schizophrenic patients (Cognitive help, 1992, p. 239).

Study Purpose

A research study is proposed to assess the appropriateness of cognitive behavioral therapy for schizophrenia. The purpose of the proposed study will be to investigate the effectiveness of cognitive behavioral therapy in the treatment of adult male patients.

Literature Review

Literature is reviewed in relation to the proposed study purpose. Literature relevant to schizophrenia, therapeutic approaches to treating schizophrenia, and cognitive behavior therapy is reviewed.

Schizophrenia

Schizophrenia is a disorder identified by the presence of "characteristic psychotic symptoms during the active phase of the illness and functioning below the highest level previously achieved..., and a duration of at least six months..." (American Psychiatric Association, 1994, p. 187). Patients suffering from the disorganized type of schizophrenia exhibit incoherence, marked loosening of associations, or grossly disorganized behavior, and flat or grossly inappropriate affect. During some phase of the illness, schizophrenia "always involves delusions, hallucinations, or certain characteristic disturbances in affect and form of thought" (p. 187). The key feature of schizophrenic delusions is a marked departure from consensual reality.

Schizophrenia is classified as subchronic when the signs of the disorder are "more or less" continuously present for at least six months, but for less than two years (American Psychiatric Association, 1994, p. 195). When the signs persist for two years or longer, the disorder is classified as chronic. Functioning below the highest level previously achieved refers to the functioning of the patient in such areas as work, social relations, and self care. When the onset of the illness is in either childhood or adolescence, functioning is related to the expected level of social development. Content of thought involves "delusions that are often multiple, fragmented, or bizarre" (p. 188). Bizarre refers to a phenomenon that in the person's culture would be regarded as totally implausible.

Form of thought refers to both a loosening of associations, and to a poverty of speech content (American Psychiatric Association, 1994, p. 188). When a loosening of associations is manifested, a patient's ideas shift from one subject to another, completely unrelated or only obliquely related subject, without the speaker's displaying any awareness that the topics are unconnected. Poverty of speech content is present when speech is adequate in amount, but conveys little information because it is vague, overly abstract, or overly concrete, repetitive, or stereotyped.

Hallucinations are major perceptual disturbances (Carpenter & Buchanan, 1994, p. 683). The most common form in schizophrenia is audio, although hallucinations may also be tactile, somatic, visual, gustatory, and olfactory in character. Affective disturbances present in schizophrenia are either flat or inappropriate. Flat refers to a virtual absence of affective expression—a monotonous voice, and an immobile face. Inappropriate refers to an affect which "is clearly discordant with the content of a person's speech or ideation" (American Psychiatric Association, 1994, p. 189).

Other aspects of the psychopathology of schizophrenia may also be present in patients suffering from the disorder. The sense of self, which provides "individuality, uniqueness, and self-direction," may be disturbed (American Psychiatric Association, 1994, p. 189). Volition disturbances (self-initiated, goal-directed activity) may grossly impair work or other role functioning. Individuals suffering from schizophrenia may also exhibit extreme difficulty in the maintenance of interpersonal relationships and in relating to the external world. At times, various psychomotor disturbances may also be present.

A diagnosis of schizophrenia requires a consideration of both general data related to the illness, and more specific data related to type (Martin, 1991, p. 921). Schizophrenia may be diagnosed if: (1) two of the following five phenomena have characterized a patient's behavior for at least one week—delusions, prominent hallucinations, incoherence, or marked loosening of associations, catatonic behavior, and flat, or grossly inappropriate affect; (2) a patient's behavior has been characterized for at least one week by bizarre delusions—the definition of bizarre delusions is intentionally not culture-free (Kendler, Spitzer, & Williams, 1989, p. 956); or (3) a patient's behavior has been characterized for at least one week by prominent hallucinations "of a voice with content having no apparent relation to depression or elation, or a voice keeping up a running commentary on the person's behavior or thoughts, or two or more voices conversing with each other" (American Psychiatric Association, 1994, p. 194).

To be diagnosed as schizophrenia, a patient's functioning must be below the highest level previously achieved and must characterize individual behavior, and the diagnosis of schizoaffective disorder and mood disorder with psychotic features must have been eliminated (Martin, 1991, p. 924). Further, it must possible to attribute the disturbance being experienced by the patient to an organic factor. When a patient has a history of autistic disorder, schizophrenia may be diagnosed only "if prominent delusions or hallucinations are also present" (American Psychiatric Association, 1994, p. 195). Paranoid schizophrenia may not be diagnosed, unless a diagnosis of both catatonic schizophrenia and disorganized schizophrenia have been rejected (Gruenberg, Kendler, & Tsuang, 1985, pp. 1356).

Therapeutic Approaches to Treating Schizophrenia

The three classes of anti psychotic drugs most often used in the treatment of schizophrenia are the phenothiazines, the thioxanthenes, and the butyrophenones (Kaplan & Sadock, 1991, p. 1207). Extrapyrmidal side effects are associated with the more potent of the phenothiazines—trifluoperazine, perphenazine, and fluphenazine. Early side effects include rigidity, restless shuffling and rocking, retrocollis, grimacing, torsion spasms, and oculogyric crises. Other major side effects which may occur include tardive dyskinesia, agranulocytosis, hepatis, rashes, and skin discolorations. Minor side effects associated with these drugs include drowsiness, dizziness, dry mouth, constipation, hypotension, anorexia, blurred vision, weight gain, breast swelling in women, lactation in women, and inhibition of ejaculation in men.

The health professional can minimize the hazards of drug therapy for schizophrenic patients by "carefully watching for side effects and recognizing the potential complications and circumstances under which side effects are most apt to occur" (Kaplan & Sadock, 1991, p. 1208). The goal in drug therapy is to use the smallest effective dose. Low dosages, however, are usually not effective in the treatment of schizophrenia. Doses are typically started at 150mg.-to-300mg. per day, and then are gradually raised to achieve a maximum anti-psychotic effect, while, at the same time, minimizing undesirable side effects. There is no evidence to support a hypothesis that "it is necessary to induce gross extrapyranidal signs in order to relieve psychosis" in the treatment of schizophrenia (p. 1205).

A substantial decrease in the incidence of recorded cases of schizophrenia has been observed since the 1960s (Eagles, 1991, p. 834). This phenomenon has led some observers to conclude that the disorder may be on the wane. Other observers, however, contend that the apparent decline in the incidence of schizophrenia may simply be the consequence of shifting treatment for the disorder to community care, wherein remission experience has been relatively high and relapse has been relatively low.

A significant reduction in the relapse rate associated with the schizophrenia disorder has also been attributed to family intervention programs (Tarrier, 1991a, pp. 475–480). Family intervention programs that instruct the relatives of patients in management and coping skills have been found to be effective in the prevention of relapse. A failure to adhere to a family intervention program or the withdrawal from such a program, however, may lead to an increase in the rate of relapse. Research has also found that costs associated with family intervention programs to minimize relapse are more than offset by reduced costs associated with the use of established mental health services; the savings approximated 27 percent (Tarrier, 1991b, pp. 481–484).

A Polish program found that drama therapy was both effective in the treatment of schizophrenia and in the minimization of relapse (Bielanska, Cechnicki, & Budzyna-Dawidowski, 1991, pp. 566–575). The goals of drama therapy are to improve patients' self-expression and knowledge of themselves and others through experiencing joint responsibility and cooperation and group feedback.

Treatment of schizophrenia with human leukocyte interferon has also been found to bring about remission of the disorder and reduce the potential for relapse (Leszek, Inglot, Cantell, & Wasik, 1991, pp. 55–63). This study found, however, that both interferon-sensitive and interferon-resistant groups exist among schizophrenics. Thus, interferon will not be effective in the treatment of all schizophrenic patients.

The findings of an Israeli study emphasized the significance of continuity in the treatment of schizophrenia (Nigal, Calev, Kugelmass, & Lerer, 1991, pp. 141–145). In this experiment, schizophrenic patients were removed from drug therapy to study side effect outcomes. Most subjects experienced relapse during the withdrawal of treatment.

Cognitive Behavioral Therapy

An assumption central to cognitive theory is that an individual's emotional and behavioral responses to events in one's life are greatly influenced by one's own interpretations and evaluations of those events (Garety, Kuipers, Fowler, & Chamberlain, 1994, p. 259). Thus, cognitive therapists are concerned with a subject's interpretation of an event, and her or his basic beliefs used in evaluating the event, regardless of perceptual accuracy.

Cognitive phenomena are grouped into three categories (Thase, Reynolds, Frank, & Simons, 1994, p. 501). The first category, referred to as automatic thoughts, is comprised of an individual's stream of consciousness thought and visual images, which occur as responses to life events. Such automatic thoughts related to events may be biased by systematic cognitive distortions. The second category is comprised of an individual's expectancies about the probabilities of responses to one's own behaviors. Such expectancies influence one's behaviors, and such expectancies are susceptible to systematic cognitive distortion. The third category of cognitive phenomena includes one's unrealistic and irrational beliefs about the nature of relationships. Such irrational beliefs, may result in dysfunctional behavioral responses. Systematic distortion related to one's automatic thoughts occurs through a variety of thought behaviors. The most frequent of these thought behaviors encountered by the cognitive analyst are over generalization—an assumption that behavior of one's is invariant, arbitrary inference—jumping to conclusions, selective abstraction—where one ignores a part of the available information, and all-or-nothing thinking—where one accepts only the extremes of a continuum as an explanation for the behavior of one's partner.

The cognitive analyst attempts to identify cognitive distortions in the automatic thoughts of a subject (Halford, 1994, p. 196). Biased attributions in one's automatic thoughts are significant because they can elicit a sense of hopelessness and helplessness regarding improvement of the problems being experienced. Expectancies involve estimates of the probabilities that will behave in certain ways in certain situations. Thus, one's expectancies influence one's own behaviors, because the tendencies is for an individual to choose actions that will most likely produce desired consequences, based on past experiences. If one's expectancies are distorted or unrealistic, however, it is less likely that appropriate behavioral choices will be made. Distorted and unrealistic expectancies are, in part, the product of one's schemata, or set of unrealistic and irrational beliefs with respect to the nature of intimate relationships. Cognitive theory holds that extreme beliefs with respect to one's self and one's interaction with one's environment are among the most important of the cognitive phenomena leading to dysfunctional behavioral responses. Basic beliefs are used by individuals in the evaluation of life event. Thus, behavior will be evaluated in the context of one's basic beliefs. If these basic beliefs are unrealistic or irrational, one's expectancies will likely also tend to be unrealistic and irrational.

Dilts, Hallbom, and Smith (1993, pp. 1–28) introduced the Neuro-Linguistic Programming (NLP) model for personal change. This model requires that the individual seeking personal change be the chief role player in effecting such change. The NLP model requires for a recognition of one's present state and a defining of one's desired state. The resource's available to the individual seeking change then provide the vehicles for moving from the present state to the desired state. The NLP model, however, also recognizes that the movement from present state to desired state can be impeded by one's limiting beliefs. The role of the analyst, thus, is to aid an individual in the gaining of the necessary understanding to overcome the individual's limiting beliefs.

Proposed Research Methodology

The proposed experimental model for the use of cognitive behavioral therapy in the treatment of schizophrenics incorporates the concepts of recognition of existing state and the defining of a desired end state. Within this context, the proposed experimental model also provides for the development by the individuals receiving treatment of an internal locus of control to assure that the recognition of existing state, defining of desired end state, and the transition process from existing state to desired end state all are controlled by the individual seeking change. The proposed experimental model also will incorporate the resources and limiting beliefs concepts. Development of the understanding required to successfully apply one's resources and to overcome one's limiting beliefs, however, will be accomplished through a process employing one's intuition, emotion, and creativity.

The proposed experimental model will be applied to a population of adult males (aged 30–40 years old) in a residential care environment who have been diagnosed as schizophrenic. Outcome measure that will be used to evaluate the experimental model are (1) change in the level of interpersonal skills, and changes in the symptomatic characteristics of schizophrenia as defined by DSM-IV.

Part V:

Schizophrenia and Psychotherapy: A Treatment Method

Schizophrenics and their families are well aware that this illness is one of the most tragic of the mental illnesses. It erodes all aspects of the patient's life, leaving them able to function only in the most basic sense. It is not terminal, however the number of sufferers who commit suicide is staggering. Medication has been found highly beneficial in alleviating many of the negative symptoms of this illness. But it cannot rebuild the social life and communication abilities of a person suffering from schizophrenia. This paper will explore the impact that psychotherapy has had on schizophrenia. First, the symptoms and occurrence of schizophrenia will be discussed. Second, the historical use of psychotherapy, and its effectiveness, will be explored. Last, several methods of psychotherapy will be explained.

Schizophrenia is actually a group of disabling conditions characterized by gross distortions of reality and withdrawal from social interaction. It also includes disorganization and fragmentations of perception, thought and emotion (Tollefson, 1996). The term "schizophrenia" means split-brain. It refers to how the thoughts and feelings may not relate to each other in a logical fashion. This split in various psychological functions is far different from another disorder, multiple personality disorder, although the two disorders have become somewhat confused by their portrayal in the media.

It is a rare disorder, as only one percent of the population, across cultures and countries, suffers from it (Larsen & Opjordsmoen, 1996; APA 1997, p. 6). Despite the low occurrence, schizophrenia tends to be expensive, accounting for 2.5 percent of all total direct health care expenditures in the United States (APA, 1997). In addition, the APA (1997) estimates that 80 percent of schizophrenics are chronically unemployed and that they account for ten percent of the totally and permanently disabled. They comprise up to 14 percent of the homeless population. Within the first year of onset, 60 percent of schizophrenics receive disability benefits. Tragically, ten percent of schizophrenics commit suicide. Clearly, "the disease of schizophrenia creates a heavy burden on multiple levels" (Rhoades, 2000, p. 258+).

Families of schizophrenics were first alerted to a problem through warning signs. These include social withdrawal, less interest in school or work, changes in appearance and hygiene, and general unusual behavior (Rhoades, 2000). Diagnoses of schizophrenia are reached through three diagnostic areas. These include characteristic symptoms, social or occupational dysfunction, and duration. A clinician would first rule out schizo-affective disorder, mood disorders, substance abuse, general medical condition, and a pervasive developmental disorder. Then he or she would look for certain symptoms over a one-month period. These symptoms would include delusions, hallucinations, disorganized speech, grossly disorganized or catatonic behavior, flat affect, lack of thought or speech fluency, and apathy (APA, 1997). Rhoades (2000) notes that this illness encompasses the entire range of human mental activity related to perception, language, emotion, and interpersonal relationships. It impedes memory, attention, and other high-level brain activities. It also dulls emotion, creates a lack of direction and purpose, and general apathy and inertia. The experience for families of watching their loved ones suffer through this illness is painful beyond words.

Experts agree that schizophrenia is fundamentally biological in nature. The patient can no more cure the illness than prevent it in the first place. However, research points to a variety of possible causes. Schizophrenia may be genetically linked, although a specific genetic marker has not been identified. Neurotransmitters have been shown to play a part in the illness as well, but characteristics found in schizophrenics are also found in healthy individuals. Generally, scientists agree that the illness is caused by a combination of both biological and environmental factors (Larsen & Opjordsmoen, 1996).

Schizophrenia has a strong tendency to run in families, as evidenced by twin studies of patients who were raised apart (Holzman, 1996). One study verified that biological children raised apart had a predictably higher incidence of schizophrenia than did foster siblings raised together. The occurrence of the illness rises from one in one hundred in the general population to one in ten in families already affected by the illness. However, the illness is not passed genetically from parents to children as dramatically and precisely as other medical illnesses, such as Huntington's Chorea and cystic fibrosis (Holzman, 1996). It is important to pursue the cause of schizophrenia in order to explore more effective therapy, medications, or possibly, a cure.

Of the mental and neurological disorders, schizophrenia is one of the most devastating. The stigma of mental illness poses an obstacle as difficult to overcome as the illness itself. The lack of understanding from society regarding mental illness has led to a marked lack of medical coverage for the illness. Many specialists feel that the lack of adequate insurance coverage is the primary reason why so few schizophrenic patients receive appropriate treatment. A secondary reason for inadequate treatment is the illness itself. It is very difficult to confront and manage. "Despite great advances in the medical treatment of schizophrenia during the second half of this century, we remain woefully deficient in our ability to deliver that treatment to patients in need. The stigma associated with mental illness is at the root of this failure and contributes to inadequacies of health insurance coverage for mental illness, lack of information and resources among the families of patients, and the difficulties many patients have in accepting their illnesses" (Dietz, 1998).

The most accepted form of treatment includes joint use of medication and therapy. The use of medication in the form of antipsychotic drugs (Kane, 1996) provides enough stability to make the use of psychological treatments effective (Rhoades, 2000). One form of therapy that has been used for schizophrenia is psychotherapy. Rosberg (2001) states that psychotherapy is neglected in the psychiatric community. It is not discussed to a great extent in publication. In addressing psychiatrists, he mentions that without active psychotherapy, they cannot possibly see the illness through patients' eyes, and thus, have no idea what their lives are like. Psychotherapists serve as sources of information, support, and help to schizophrenics. The therapist becomes familiar with the patient's view of his or her illness, and works with the patient from that point of view.

Therapists provide a safe means of communication about the nature and cause of the illness and the need for drug treatment (Harvard, 2001). For example, if a patient complains about hearing voices, the therapist will ask questions about them. When the therapist learns when and where the voices emerge, how often and for how long they "visit," what precipitates their appearance, and how the patient feels about them, the therapist can begin work with the patient to control them. The patient may learn methods for turning the voices off. By using this method, the therapist effectively teaches the patient that the voices are created by his or her illness, and that he or she can control them (Harvard, 2001). In essence, "even if the psychotic episodes are not completely eliminated, this sense of control may greatly reduce the influence of hallucinations and delusions, relieving anger, anxiety, and depression" (Harvard, 2001).

Psychotherapy has been used in many forms in the past century. Today, many methods are used successfully. In institutional settings, contemporary psychiatric units all have forms of group psychotherapy. Depending on length of stay, psychotherapists are challenged to set group goals and modify techniques for the broad range of patients in each group. Therapists will choose methods such as focused goals, closed memberships, and homogenous groups of patients based on symptoms or levels of psychological functioning (Beeber, 1991). A team group format is often used with schizophrenic patients. The disadvantages to this method include that it is formatted to assist the lowest functioning member. This may cause it to be meaningless to higher functioning patients. Alternatively, formatting the psychotherapy for the needs of the high functioning members leaves the rest of the group exposed to stress and anxiety (Beeber, 1991). Advantages of the team group method include that the members benefit from the presence of the group. It functions somewhat like a small community within the hospital. Beeber states, "the small group reflects the interpersonal interactions characteristic of the unit as a whole and can provide an opportunity in a more supportive and structured environment for patients to understand their hospital experience, spot problems in relating to others and begin the process of changing maladaptive ways of relating (1991, p. 78+).

Other advantages include the fact that more psychotic patients can provide meaningful feedback to higher functioning patients. Interestingly, patients with few symptoms are often in denial about their illness, placing them at extreme risk. Patients currently suffering from many symptoms are often in touch with the emotional themes of the group. This insight has shown to be very useful (Beeber, 1991). Also, the team group format provides a safe environment for schizophrenics to offer help to each other. This is often the first time the patients experience altruism. Beeber (1991) acknowledges the disadvantages of this form of therapy, but given the strong advantages, he encourages psychiatric units to use several group formats to compensate.

Many philosophies of psychotherapeutic treatment have evolved since schizophrenia was first named as a mental illness. In the early 1960's, doctors used a method known as intensive psychotherapy. Practitioners of psychoanalysis created this method. It involved psychological investigation, behavior insight, and emotional experience with the therapist (Schulz, 1975; as cited in Rhoades, 2000). The assumption is that clients can make changes in themselves outside the therapeutic setting (Rhoades, 2000). Psychotherapy necessitates involvement of the entire family rather than the patient only. Therapists commonly educate families regarding the illness and its management, avoids placing blame, instill hope, and assist them with taking a long-term perspective (Mueser, 1996).

Family therapists and counselors developed the second type of psychotherapy. It applies solution-focused interventions to the treatment of mental illness. Therapists who use this method adapt elements of psychosocial rehabilitation, education, and skill building to their treatment protocol. Therapy involves learning and reinforcement of problem-solving skills. Therapists who utilize these techniques hope that medications alleviate the presence of hallucinations and bizarre behavior, while therapy assists with the absence of social skills and motivation (Rhoades, 2000). Today, those who practice psychotherapy with schizophrenics tend to use a practical, person-centered method, rather than one that follows a particular school of thought. According to Rhoades (2000), the family psychotherapy approach should make a successful impact on the coping skills of the family, teach communication, and encourage the development of extended social support. Families can learn to help with medication adherence, decrease substance abuse, and manage stress.

Kates and Rockland (1994) noted that the current use of psychopharmacology, social skills training, vocational rehabilitation, and family intervention is far from comprehensive. Instead, this treatment plan is missing two vital elements. First, a coordinator of services with a commitment to the family is necessary for successful treatment. Second, a treatment plan for schizophrenia is not complete without dynamic psychotherapy. In a review of literature, they found that many studies of traditional psychotherapy produced poor results. Several studies found that drugs alone worked as well as a regime of both psychotherapy and drugs together. A study produced by Stanton and Gunderson in 1984 appears to have halted the use of dynamic psychotherapy for many years subsequent to publication. These researchers found that other forms of therapy were as effective as insight-oriented psychotherapy. Because psychotherapy is expensive and time-consuming to administer, Kates and Rockland (1994) make the point that a few key studies caused cessation of the use of psychotherapy in general for schizophrenic patients.

Studies that refute these findings, and support the use of psychotherapy, include a meta-analysis of studies of psychotic patients treated with drug therapy alone and patients treated with a dual method of drugs and psychotherapy. The results show an effect size of .5 for drugs only compared to .8 for a combined therapy regime (Kates & Rockland, 1994).

It can be argued that different types of psychotherapy exist, and some may be more effective for schizophrenics than others. The studies refuting the effectiveness of such therapy were exploring a traditional method. Kates and Rockland (1994) assert that psychodynamic supportive therapy has experienced significant advances in the past two decades. They state that, "the discouraging outcomes of studies of intensive psychotherapy have led to an over reactive retreat from all dynamic psychotherapy for these patients" (Kates & Rockland, 1994, p. 543+).

The method they perceive as most effective is Psycho-dynamically Oriented Supportive Therapy (POST). This method is based on ego psychology, where the goals are to strengthen the ego functions, both directly and indirectly. The therapist using this technique assumes a verbally active role that tends to be more self-revealing than in other methods. Therapists will interject some of their own realities and values, and will closely monitor both positive and negative transferences by the patient. Resistances and defenses that would lead to maladaptive behavior are confronted and discouraged immediately. Positive changes in behavior are immediately supported, encouraged, and strengthened. This method does not utilize free association and dream analysis because the focus is on the conscious (Kates & Rockland, 1994).

Treatment of a schizophrenic patient using POST is divided into three phases. The first is inpatient, where the patient functions so poorly that hospitalization is necessary. The second is the stabilization phase. Treatment during this phase focuses on building a therapeutic alliance, psychoeducation of the patient and family, and determining the appropriate medication regimen. This is the appropriate time for the therapist to foster a trusting relationship with the patient. Strong positive alliances with patients have been shown to be "associated with decreased neuroleptic, increased compliance, and improved clinical state" (Kates & Rockland, 1994, p. 543+).

The third phase is the maintenance phase. At this point, the therapist urges the therapy along to represent a supportive therapy common to healthy patients. Medication may be shifted to lower dose strategies. Psycho-education is continued with both patients and family as clinically appropriate. More ambitious family work might be considered, such as working on unhealthy family dynamics. Social skills training and vocational rehabilitation are used when needed. In treating schizophrenics, a psychotherapist will never terminate treatment altogether. Instead, the patient and therapist may reach a consensus that active treatment is no longer necessary. In this case, meetings will continue every three months for purposes of monitoring psychological health.

In a review of research on supportive psychotherapy, Conte (1994) argues that better specification of the treatment, and appropriate objective assessment techniques are needed before comparisons of this therapy can be made to other forms of therapy. He notes that the goals, strategies, and techniques of the approach have been better defined in recent years, but studies cannot support any increase in quality of the program. At the time of his study, Conte (1994) mentions that supportive psychotherapy had become the most common form of psychotherapy used for patients experiencing acute crisis, and for patients with chronic psychopathology who show severe and persistent ego deficits and defects.

Those who practice supportive psychotherapy disagree on its definition. Some view it as similar to dynamic, insight-oriented therapy, and perceive it as a subcategory of psychoanalysis. Others view it as its own philosophy, where specific techniques and interventions are used. In reality, the point becomes irrelevant in practice, where therapists from both sides of the issue tend to mix a variety of methods to achieve the same result. All patients are different, and require a different approach to treatment, regardless of the philosophy of their treating therapist. In summary, Conte (1994) notes, "supportive therapy generally focuses on symptom relief and overt behavior change through support of the patients' adaptive mechanisms and environmental resources" (p. 494+).

Conte agrees that the strategies of supportive therapy are highly effective. These include a substantial effort by the therapist to support the patient through a strong relationship, as well as focusing on conscious material, openly acknowledging and accepting the patient's methods of adaptation, encouraging positive behaviors, suggestion, persuasion, ventilation, giving advice, setting limits, testing reality, reassurance, and serving as a model (1994).

A study conducted in 1986 explored comparative studies of supportive psychotherapy with other dynamic therapies. The results showed that as compared to psychoanalysis, the patients treated with supportive psychotherapy fared far better. The conclusions stated, "results obtained using supportive techniques were far more impressive than had originally been anticipated, while the results of psychoanalytic treatments were less impressive than had been predicted" (Conte, 1994, p. 494). Additionally, the researchers asserted that all treatments tend to become more supportive over time, and that patients' progress is associated with supportive intervention.

Honig (1991) describes a specific action psychotherapeutic technique that he developed specifically to alleviate chronic hallucinations. Studies show that schizophrenics most often experience auditory hallucinations, commonly in the form of voices. The content tends to be threatening and antagonistic. Patients usually deny them out of fear, as it is estimated that 80 percent of hallucinations are destructive or self-deprecating, while the other 20 percent tend to be seductively flattering, supportive, or instructive (Honig, 1991).

A new form of psychotherapy being explored is known as direct confrontation. It is designed to permeate the patient's maladaptive behavior and perspective, and disrupt the psychosis. Then different sets of behavior are produced that are more strategic in terms of the expectations of society. According to Rosberg (2001, previous methods are too passive. Psychotherapy cannot work unless the therapist takes an active and persuasive approach. Direct confrontation can be seen as forceful intervention, as the therapist may choose to use a firm tone of voice to communicate through the patient's defenses. However this is the only way to make patients aware of behaviors that lead to debilitating regressive reactions, and educating them about how those behaviors affect other people. Rosberg (2001) further explains that the therapist must be stronger than the overwhelming symptoms of the illness.

Training for psychotherapy is inconsistent, according to Rosberg (2001). It cannot be learned from books alone, but must be a dynamic process involving both the student and teacher. Both people must actively observe each other administering therapy. Psychotherapy should not be a secretive process conducted by doctors in private. This makes therapy virtually ineffective, especially in institutions, because the staff and support system cannot support the ideas discussed in therapy. On the other hand, Dr. Rosberg has found that therapy conducted in front of the staff and the therapist's supervisor help all parties involved. The therapist grows professionally, the patient feels supported, and the staff has a better idea of what happens in therapy. This "living room therapy" can continue to the point at which the patient requests private meetings. Rosberg (2001) emphasizes that veteran schizophrenics (rather than "chronic") have the potential for change under the right conditions.

People who suffer from schizophrenia undoubtedly face enormous obstacles in battling the illness. The cause of the illness has not been discovered, and is likely the product of many factors. Treating physicians must focus on the individual, and choose a course of treatment that proves most effective. Medications are a necessary component of treatment, but schizophrenics cannot fully recover without a nurturing form of psychotherapy. This form of therapy has been shown to be effective in the treatment of schizophrenia. Furthermore, some methods are more effective than others. Methods that insist on a strong relationship between the patient and the therapist, and that emphasize the need for the therapist to insist on behavioral change appear most effective. Traditional psychotherapy that is impersonal and impassive does not offer as strong a treatment as more contemporary methods. As research continues, perhaps the field of psychiatry will explore more humanistic means of training to further the development of psychotherapy for use in treating schizophrenia.

Part VI:

Prostaglandins and Schizophrenia: Hype or Hope? The pharmacology of Prostaglandins and Schizophrenia

Abstract

There is a growing body of evidence that abnormalities of the cell membrane, particularly depletion of n-3 & n-6 essential fatty acids (EFA/Prostaglandins) are found in patients suffering from schizophrenia. Prostaglandins are found in the brain and are involved in modulation of nerve conduction, neurotransmitter release and post-synaptic transmitter actions. Essential fatty acids, constitution about 20% of the dry weight of the brain, are precursors of prostaglandin. Certain observations in schizophrenia suggest and aetiological link between schizophrenia, essential fatty acids and prostaglandins.

Thus, lipid neuro-chemistry is now an important focus in schizophrenia research. Reports of abnormalities in brain lipids in schizophrenia appear widely within the medical and lay press. Disordered brain fatty acid metabolism was first postulated to play a part in pathophysiology of schizophrenia by Horrobin (1977) and lately there is evidence that new treatments could follow.

I will attempt to review clinical research on abnormalities in membrane fatty acid metabolism and therapeutic trails of fatty acids in schizophrenia. I will also discuss the psychopharmacology of EFA, how they work on the brain to improve symptoms-inclusive of any clinical trials, research, and testing that has been done on the subject. I will then conclude my own hypothesis on the future of this possible treatment and cure for schizophrenia.

Schizophrenia Redefined: The Pharmacology of Prostaglandins and Schizophrenia

Schizophrenia Redefined

Mental illness is a subject that is for the most part neglected in political and social arenas in the United States. Despite the numbers of people affected by mental illness, people diagnosed with a disorder are not provided the same support, financial or otherwise, that is afforded patients with other, more physical, illnesses. Mental illness remains a taboo subject in our society because, despite medical research to the contrary, the general public believes that these people brought a mental illness on themselves through their behavior or thoughts. In reality, mental illness is very much a biochemical disorder. Studies show that mental illness is cause by many factors that are biological in nature, such as a chemical dysfunction in the brain. Of the mental illnesses listed in the Diagnostic And Statistical Manual Of Mental Disorders (DSM-IV) (APA 285+), nine of them are major psychotic disorders, including schizophrenia.

Many biochemical causes of schizophrenia have been theorized recently. Some researchers have studied abnormalities of dopamine metabolism in brains of schizophrenic patients. Another area of focus has been glutamaterigic transmission, another area of brain neurotrans-mitters. More recent studies show compelling evidence that abnormal brain development, caused by low maternal weight at conception or exposure to the influenza virus in utero, is associated with later onset of schizophrenia (Mukherjee & Mahadik, 1994).

However, an area of study that has grown steadily in recent years shows that abnormalities with cell membranes is highly correlated with development of schizophrenia. Depleted levels of n-3 and n-6 essential fatty acids (EFA/Prostaglandins), have been shown to occur in significant numbers of schizophrenic patients. Prostaglandins, which are found in the brain, are involved in modulation of nerve conduction, neurotransmitter release and post-synaptic transmitter actions. Essential fatty acids (EFA's) are precursors to prostaglandins, and constitute about 20 percent of the dry weight of the brain. The body of research involved with the study of the relationship between EFA's and schizophrenia has found an aetiological link between them, along with prostaglandins. In discussing lipid neurochemistry in relation to schizophrenia, first a literature review will be conducted. Next, the psychopharmacology of EFA's will be discussed along with the effects of medication on schizophrenia symptoms. Finally, the future of this body of research will be discussed.

Weston Price, a pioneer in the area of nutrition, discovered the benefits of EFA's in the 1930's. His research led him to understand that organ meat, or insects in cultures without a meat supply, were highly valued food items in nearly all cultures. He began treating patients with a combination of cod liver oil and butter oil. Together these substances seemed to quickly revive patients. Dr. Price did not have the technology to discover why the oils were so beneficial, but the answer is that high vitamin butter is rich in arachindonic acid (AA) and other substances needed for the omega-6 pathway. Cod liver oil is rich in EPA needed for the omega-3 pathway. Also, the saturated fatty acids in butter help the unsaturated fatty acids in cod liver oil work more effectively (Fallon & Enig, 1999).

Horrobin is thought by experts in the field to be the first researcher to make the connection between lipids and schizophrenia. He explains that one of the processes that differentiate apes from humans is change in lipid metabolism. Neuronal micro-connectivity is partially regulated by phospholipid synthesizing, remodeling, and degrading enzymes (Horrobin, 1999). The richness of neuronal connectivity is likely to be related to creativity. The occurrence of schizophrenia may be related to abnormalities of phospholipid breakdown and synthesis, which would affect synaptic connectivity. Adoption studies show that relatives of schizophrenics are at high risk of developing schizophrenia. However, they also display exceptional creativity at levels above normal for the population. Horrobin concludes, "the changes in phospholipid metabolism which are associated with schizophrenia may also be responsible for those features characteristic of our humanity" (1999, p. 5255).

Recent discoveries about schizophrenia concur with Horrobin's lipid hypothesis. First, people with schizophrenia are more likely than control groups to have a depletion of arachidonic acid (AA) and docosahexaenoic acid (DHA) in red blood cell membranes. Second, patients with the illness have an increased rate of breakdown of phospholipids in the cerebral cortex. Finally, patients display an increase in phospholipase (PLA2) activity. Thus, "schizophrenic symptoms may result from excessive PLA2 activity leading to depletion of the phospholipids AA and DHA in red blood cell membranes (Hillbrand, Spitz, & VandenBos, 1997).

One of the first studies in this area extracted phospholipids from plasma samples in both schizophrenic and control patients. The researchers found that the levels of phospholipids were the same across both groups, but the amounts of fatty acids in the phospholipids was significantly different. The n-6 EFA levels were significantly lower than the control group, while the n-3 EFA levels were higher. In specific, linoleic acid and arachidonic acid were significantly reduced in all three patient groups, and two groups showed lower levels of dihomogamma-linolenic acid. The researchers acknowledge that the difference may be due to differences in EFA metabolism for schizophrenic patients. They may also be due to the effects of prolonged institutionalization, prolonged drug therapy, or diet (Horrobin, Manku, Morse-Fisher, Vaddadi, Courtney, Glen, Glen, Spellman, & Bates, 1989).

Another early study analyzed forskolin-stimulation in the intact platelets of 32 schizophrenics and 30 normal controls in an effort to relate transducing mechanisms with schizophrenia. Results showed that cyclic 3', 5'—adenosine monophosphate (cAMP) response after forskolin-stimulation was significantly lower in the test group than the control group. This result supports the theory that impaired adenylate cyclase activity leads to PGE1 hyposensitivity in platelets of schizophrenic patients (Ofuji, Kaiya, Nosaki, & Tsurami, 1989).

A study in 1991 compared the brains of seven schizophrenic patients with seven control brains. The researchers found significant abnormalities in the frontal cortex of the study group, and the abnormalities formed a pattern. Results showed that the abnormalities "were most strikingly seen in the composition of PE, the PL fraction that is by far the richest in EFA's" (Horrobin, Manku, Hillman, Iain, & Glen, 1991, p. 800). Evidence already exists that the cerebral cortex metabolizes fatty acids differently, and that the two sides of the cortex may also behave differently with regard to EFA metabolism. The researchers recommend further study to determine if the metabolism of EFA's in the brains of schizophrenic patients affects the pathogenesis of the disease (Horrobin et al., 1991).

In exploring whether schizophrenics share this same depletion of EFA's with other mentally ill individuals, researchers in 1991 compared the two groups. The researchers note that in studies of plasma fatty acids of schizophrenic patients in the United States, England, Scotland, Ireland, and Japan, only Linoleic Acid is found to be abnormal across all countries, as is it's relationship to its metabolites. The difference in the levels of this fatty acid in the study group and the control group is small, but is made more valid by the fact that normal brains and those brains of patients with affective disorder had no difference in levels (Kaiya, Horrobin, Manku, & Fisher, 1991).

In 1991, Vaddadi studied the use of gamma-linolenic acid in the treatment of schizophrenia and tardive dyskinesia (TD), or abnormal involuntary movements. Results of EFA supplementation did not show significant improvement in the rate of TD, but did show improvement on mental state measurements and Weschler memory scale scores. Vaddadi suggests that more accurate dosing may provide better results for TD, but claims the results of the study lay the groundwork for research into EFA supplementation for treatment of schizophrenia (1991).

After the publication of the study mentioned above, Vaddadi initiated a study to assess the relationship between psychiatric status, TD, and levels of the n-3 and n-6 EFA's in red blood cell membranes and plasma. The study took place over four and a half years, and was published in 1996. Patients did not show lower levels of n-6 and n-3 series EFA's than the control group, as predicted. Results did show that lower levels of linoleic acid and higher levels of dihomogamma-linolenic acid were found in the schizophrenic patients as compared to the control group. Patient's EFA profiles varied widely. The researchers maintain, "it is possible that the majority of chronic schizophrenics have an inherent difficulty in incorporating EFA's into neural membranes thus affecting brain development and increasing their vulnerability to develop super-sensitivity to neuroleptics and TD" (Vaddadi, Gilleard, Soosai, Polonowita, Gibson, & Burrows, 1996). They also postulate as to the effects of abnormalities with EFA's on the dopaminergic receptor function (Vaddadi et al., 1996).

Schizophrenia has formally been attributed to the dysfunction of neurotransmitters. However, a model that emphasizes abnormalities in lipid metabolism better explains at least eight characteristics of the illness. Abnormalities in neurotransmitter function do not explain the facts that schizophrenics are relatively free of inflammatory disorders, have a high pain threshold, and their symptoms subside when they have a fever. Patients with schizophrenia have an increased rate of perinatal viral infections and other perinatal problems. It is more prevalent in men than in women, but occurs in equal numbers worldwide, although significant variability in severity has been noted. Finally, stress has been shown to precipitate onset of the illness (Hillbrand, Spitz, & VandenBos, 1997).

The nature of this research lends clinicians to postulate as to whether supplements of EFA's will alleviate the symptoms of schizophrenia. No clinician is so optimistic as to assume that a supplement of one substance will cure an illness of this complexity, but this research could greatly assist in the treatment of the illness.

One study verified that the difference in cross-cultural occurrences of schizophrenia was accounted for by the nature of dietary fat intake.

Industrialized western countries had higher occurrence than developing countries such as India (Mukherjee & Mahadik, 1994). Additionally, a study conducted by Dr. Malcolm Peet correlated dietary omega-3 fatty acid levels with the severity of schizophrenic symptoms. He found significant clinical improvement in treatment-resistant patients, and eicosapentaenoic acid (EPA) was more effective than DHA as an adjunct to antipsychotic medication (Bender, 1998).

Some studies are using fish oil or primrose oil as the source of omega-3 fatty acids. One study supplemented patients' diets with Max EPA fish oil for six weeks. Following the change in diet scores on the Positive and Negative Syndrome Scale and the Abnormal Involuntary Movement Scale were significantly improved (Mellor, Laugharne, & Peet, 1995). In a follow-up study, the same researchers found a similar result, but also verified that only positive symptoms of the illness improved significantly, as compared to negative symptoms. In addition, supplementation was related to a significant change in membrane fatty acids and a significant increase in red blood cell membrane levels of EPA (Mellor, Laugharne, & Peet, 1996).

Another study tested both fish oil and primrose oil and found a positive effect of EPA in trial groups. The researcher suggests that use of EPA may help people avoid use of standard antipsychotic drugs. No effects of primrose oil were found (Joy, Mumby-Croft, & Joy, 2000). In order to determine the therapeutic potential of EFA supplementation, researchers need to design randomized clinical trials that measure the long-term effects. As stated by Fenton, Hibbein, & Knable (1999), "independent replication confirming a significant benefit of EPA supplementation will trigger a major effort to understand its pathophysiologic significance and mechanism of action in schizophrenia" (p. 17).

In order to find a cure for schizophrenia, several strides in research must be made. First, molecular genetic techniques will allow future scientists to pinpoint the exact location on the human gene for predisposition to schizophrenia, and perhaps also the source for brain lipid metabolism. This would possibly provide the opportunity to control for this illness, or at least cure it on an individual basis. Second, although the research in this area is suggestive at best, and far from conclusive, as studies continue, manufacturers of omega-3 and other EFA supplements should work to produce a pure, consistent, measurable product. Currently, such substances are uncontrolled, which is a dangerous situation for a schizophrenic individual ultimately hoping to use EFA's as a treatment option (Bender, 1998). Last, future research will approach this issue with a holistic philosophy. It will examine the role of lipids in all psychological functioning. Any existing links between neurodevelopmental processes and cognition, depression, aggression and all psychiatric illnesses will be explored (Hillbrand, Spitz, & VandenBos, 1997).

There is a growing body of evidence that abnormalities of the cell membrane are found in patients who suffer from schizophrenia. Particularly, depletion of n-3 and n-6 EFA's are significantly lower in schizophrenic individuals. Research studies continue to explore this area and examine why the EFA's are depleted, in what structures they are missing, and which EFA's most effect the symptoms of the illness. Clinicians are testing the effects of supplementation of various EFA's to assess their effect on schizophrenia symptoms. Schizophrenia is such a complex illness that it is doubtful a cure will be found. However, research in this area might eventual produce evidence that this illness can be controlled using natural EFA's. Subsequently a form of treatment may be developed that greatly improves the lives of people who suffer from this illness.

Part VII:

Personal Stories

Stories:

http://www.zeta.org.au/~puma/mm
Misty Mirror

Personal Story I: MISTY'S STORY

My childhood

My older brother often brutalised me. I screamed from pain. My mother didn't protect me from him. Instead she labelled me a 'bad' boy and sent me to my father for punishment. I screamed and raged. Once my brother tried to bugger me.

To make things worse, my mother doted on my brother. With me she usually was abrupt and irritable. When I challenged her about her bias, she told me that I was mad. She never hugged me nor told me that she loved me. She often criticised and punished me for my behaviour, thoughts and feelings. I rarely received praise. She didn't take any interest in my play or my relationships. Whether I talked to my mother calmly, cried, or screamed at her, made no difference to her appearance. When I tried to oppose her, she sent me to my father for punishment.

She regularly cooked our meals, washed our clothes and cleaned the family home. She was meticulous.

My father rarely talked to me. He was only interested in my mother, his work, his house, his pets and his garden. He was a workaholic. He often raged at me and hit me. I was terrified of him.

My father supported us financially. He operated a small business. He worked hard.

On Christmas eves my parents decorated a Christmas tree and gave us presents. I enjoyed annual visits to the sideshow. My parents bought liquorice for my brother and me. We were allowed to go on the Big Dipper. On rare occasions we children were allowed to play cards with my parents. My brother did not hurt me when he was supervised.

My Teenage Years

When I was 13 years old, my parents, my brother and I migrated from Germany to Australia. In my school I was called Hitler and a Nazi. I was taunted. I couldn't discuss this problem at home. I was not a fighter. I was unable to ignore the abuse. I felt fear, pain and shame. I thought that I had to prove that Germans were not fools. I set out to get good results in my schoolwork. Luckily the teachers were good to me. At the end of the year I got the top aggregate marks in my class. The other children started to talk to me civilly. I was able to make a friend. I had won.

In my final year I was dux of my school. I decided to seek a university education because I thought that that impressed the girls. Because my memory isn't good, I had forgotten that I had only excelled at my academic work to prove to the Australian children that Germans were not fools. I had achieved that.

I had spent most of my highschool years studying. It had been stressful. My health had suffered.

Friends

I only learned to make friends when I was 19 years old.

Two years later I started copying my father's aggressive behaviour and my brother's bullying. My friends put up with this for a year—then they abandoned me. I was devastated.

My Love Life

I was a loner. At the age of 18 years I was attracted to a popular girl at school. I had a few dates with her. After that she told me that she had no time for me. I misunderstood the motives of the girl. I thought that she loved me, but found our relationship too painful. Actually she already had a boyfriend.

I felt guilty for not satisfying her "yearning". I didn't know that I was deluded. I also wanted her to mother me. I tried to repair the relationship.

After a couple of months the girl told me to leave her alone. I thought that she was moody. I believed that she rejected me when she felt pain and anger. I thought that when she was calm, she wanted me to "fix" the relationship. Unknowingly I pestered the girl.

I was in a "double bind". I felt extreme pain.

I thought that I saw the girl talk to her friends about me. I also thought she talked about me to her parents, relatives and neighbours. I thought that these people felt that we belonged together and that they tried to "fix" our relationship.

Later I thought that I was so important that all the children at school and all the people in the neighbouring suburbs were talking about us. I thought they all tried to get us together again.

Later still, when I started university, I thought the "talking" spread to everyone at the university. After that, when I moved to other cities in Australia, I thought the "talking" spread to the other cities in Australia.

Fortunately after two years I realised that the "talking" was a delusion. I felt extremely relieved.

When I was 22 years and 34 years old, I had two similar relationships with women. Both times the women rejected me after a short relationship. Both times I thought that they really loved me. Fortunately, however, I did not imagine that everyone tried to 'fix' our relationship.

I thought that the three relationships were "love". I thought that my more ordinary relationships, which were much less emotional, were not "right". Hence I broke them off.

University

I was ambitious. At the age of 19 years I enrolled at a university in a bachelor degree course. I suffered from delusions relating to my first girl friend. I found that and the stress of the studying to great and abandoned my course after two months.

A year later I enrolled in a similar degree course in a university in another Australian city. I passed all the examinations. I was awarded some credits. Three years later I graduated. My parents did not come to my graduation. My friends showed little interest. I still didn't have an appropriate relationship with a young woman. I was disappointed.

Work

Because I had a university education, I was channelled into difficult jobs. I found the work stressful. Sometimes I coped badly.

A Demonstration

When I was 24 years old, young political activists told me how policemen had hurt them during demonstrations.

I felt sympathetic. I believed that the police should behave fairly.

One day I was bored. I went into the city to watch a demonstration. It became violent. I saw a policeman grabbing a man and throwing him along the road.

Now that I had a university degree, I thought that I was a leader in society. I thought that I had to correct the police officer. I tried to stop him from behaving "inappropriately" by threatening him with violence.

I was arrested, tried, committed and jailed.

I thought that there was no justice in society. I felt crazy.

I started to perceive hallucinations and had delusions of grandeur—I was crazy. I couldn't cope any more. I checked into a psychiatric hospital. Three months later I was discharged on medication. I had contracted schizophrenia and depression.

A Mentor

When I was 25 years old, I met an older person who took an interest in me. He was an artist and actor. He expressed care for me. I could see it on his face. My parents and my brother had never expressed such care. The mentor also took an interest in my friends and my colleagues. My parents and my brother had never expressed such interest. The mentor also showed me that he could read the character of my friends. I had never met anyone who could do that. I learned to respect him. He said that I was a "good" person. He increased my self-esteem. I felt joy and excitement.

My mentor spoke badly of doctors and the "drugs" that they prescribe. He said that many patients in psychiatric hospitals are "normal". He influenced me. On several occasions I stopped taking my medication. Each time I had a psychotic episode.

Recent Times

When I was forty years old, a new psychiatrist taught me to trust the medication that doctors prescribe. I learned that my mentor knew about art and could read people's characters, but was not an expert in the domain of medicine. Now my schizophrenia is controlled and my depression is reduced with appropriate medication.

In GROW groups, an Australian mental health organisation, I learned that I am not alone. There are people who suffered similarly. Also in the GROW groups I learned to increase my self-esteem.

At Co-Dependents Anonymous meetings I got to know myself better. I "divorced" my family of origin for two years. Also at Co-Dependents Anonymous meetings I learned to help myself and to help those that seek assistance, but to refrain from giving unsolicited help.

From reading psychology books, self help books and by writing a journal, I learned better ways of relating to women.

I learned to joke.

Now I sometimes have comfortable feelings, sometimes uncomfortable ones and sometimes I feel serene.

The Future

I want to grow closer to my Higher Power.

I want to finish "working" the Twelve Steps of Recovery from Co-Dependents Anonymous.

I want to have friendships and a better relationship.

I want to do part-time charitable work.

I want to continue saving for my retirement.

Personal Story II: IAN'S STORY

(www.chovil.com)

I have schizophrenia and have been on medication now since 1990, the length of time I have lived in Canada. I'm 48 and my schizophrenia started in late adolescence. I struggled for ten years between 1980 and 1990, quite delusional, and very poor. I eventually got in trouble with the law and received three years probation with the condition that I see a psychiatrist for those three years. I've been to jail, been actively alcoholic, attempted suicide, and been homeless. My story illustrates an interplay of biology and sociology that can make schizophrenia a devastating illness. There is the illness itself, and the way we, as a society, treat people who develop it.

There is good cause for optimism though. The atypical medications are more effective with fewer side effects. There is growing recognition of the value of early intervention and relapse prevention. The public is developing an interest in schizophrenia. These three trends promise a far less destructive schizophrenia then what I had to experience.

A Brief History

Schizophrenia can come on rather suddenly around age 18 in men and 25 in women or it can have an insidious, meaning gradual onset. My schizophrenia seemed to start when I was about 17–18 although I was not a well adjusted teenager before that. I developed my first major romantic relationship at 17 which gradually deteriorated over the next four years. With an insidious onset you gradually lose your relationships with friends, family and lovers, as your symptoms increase and you end up quite alone. My mother says now that she noticed a change around 18, that I lost all my ambition to suceed. When I was sixteen I scored in the top three percentile in a province wide mathematics contest, and my favorite subjects were math and physics. By the time I was eighteen I had lost interest in school and only applied to university because my father was so insistent I go. I was quite strange from 18–25 at high school and university and thought I needed psychological therapy along the lines of Gestalt therapy or Rolfing. I was a very rebellious teenager who experienced a lot of emotional turmoil. One significant indication of schizophrenia was my inability to plan my future. I took courses that sounded interesting, smoked a lot of marijuana and drank too much at parties. I was notably incapable of and uninterested in long term romantic relationships and in fact was very anxious in any kind of social situation. I doubt that any psychiatrist would have been able to diagnose schizophrenia at that point though. I graduated with an Hon B.Sc. from Trent University with a double major in biology and anthropology. I applied to one graduate school at the last minute as I realized that my degree was not a career and was accepted.

At graduate school in Nova Scotia in 1978 I kept going to the university clinic about my physical health, afraid that my health was going to fall apart, that I had picked up a form of syphyllis that couldn't be detected by standard lab tests, etc. I was referred to a psychiatrist and before long I was hospitalized for a couple of weeks. What started as having an analyst like Woody Allen became an involuntary hospitalization. I had some delusions that Jim Jones, who was responsible for 500 people committing suicide en masse, was trying to force me to commit suicide but I never told anyone. I was getting pretty confused though. Unfortunately no one mentioned schizophrenia to me or my father, who is a physician, and I thought I had just had some sort of nervous breakdown. I saw someone after I was discharged about once a month for a few months. I remember taking Chlorpromazine before I was hospitalized which I didn't like and some Stellazine after I was discharged. My father encouraged me to take it but I was scared of it and I only took it for a little while. The medication seemed to cause my delusions and I believed that for many years.

My father convinced me to try and finish my year even though I wanted to drop out. It was a very miserable year for me. Some courses went unfinished and I was kicked out of graduate school. I worked for a summer in Toronto, the fall in London, and then I headed out west to Vancouver Island. I knew someone there in a small pulp mill town called Crofton but he moved up island and I rented an apartment in the strip joint tavern, alone again.

As I relapsed I had mostly delusions and paranoia. I thought the CIA was after me for awhile after I wrote a letter to the editor of Science magazine about how the US military was using dioxin as a weapon in Vietnam. My delusions had faded for the previous summer but they had never completely disappeared. That is to say I believed some pretty strange things. In Halifax I thought I had discovered the cause of World War Two. The influenza epidemic of 1918 changed peoples' nervous systems so the cause of the war was a neurovirus. I thought my law professor in Halifax was very well connected with influential people in world politics and was telling people about my theory. Various important people were coming from Europe to meet the man who discovered the cause of World War 2. So for example someone might come up to me in Crofton and talk about mopeds and I would think this man was the president of Motobecane, the world's largest manufacturer of mopeds. People seemed to know me before I introduced myself, and the local townspeople seemed to be laughing at me. I remember once the political cartoon in the local paper seemed to be about me and people who picked me up hitchiking seemed to know who I was.

In the spring of 1980 I left Crofton forced out by the townspeople who demanded I get a job. I took the bus with no destination in mind until I ran out of money. From then on I usually hitchiked, mostly through Alberta and B.C. quitting a job with my first pay check because I found working with people so difficult. They were playing games with me and making fun of me. I would then hitchike somewhere else. I thought I was being followed by a WW2 veteran everywhere I went who wanted me to shape up by working in construction like he did after the war. I kept trying to escape him but he had friends everywhere. I slept in city parks, by the side of the road and in single men's hostels. I was homeless and often penniless.

I remember once in Calgary staying at the single men's hostel and not getting to eat very much for several weeks, becoming quite weak. I couldn't work because I had dioxin poisining and this was affecting my cortical hormone balance making work too stressful. Tibetan buddhist lamas were reading my mind everywhere I went in Calgary, respectful and curious, because I had caused the Mt. St. Helen's erruption for them earlier that year through tantric meditation.

I don't think I quite understood or believed what was happening to me, but I was determined not to admit defeat and return to my parents house. It seemed like I had powerful friends who wanted me to pull myself up by my bootstraps. Only two years earlier I had been in graduate school, with a new friend, David Rae, discussing world politics while watching the CBC news at a local bar. David's brother, Bob Rae, later became the Premier of Ontario.

Come late fall I was in Victoria, driven south by the approaching winter. There I was somehow able to pay rent and I stayed there for four years. I started studying Tibetan buddhism and took refuge in the lama who lived there, Tashi Namjyal. I thought he was capable of all kinds of supernatural powers of the mind like telepathy and telekinesis. It is a tremendous invasion of privacy to have someone reading your mind all the time uninvited. I believed he was controling my dreams while I slept as well. He said to me in his broken English, "you special" and I thought that meant I had a lot of natural ability to be a very powerful tantric like him. He was the equivalent of a graduate teacher in the Tibetan monastic system.

I had caused the Mt. St. Helen's eruption with his guidance through tantric meditation. I had bad karma so I wasn't given control or access to my power but by causing Mt. St. Helen's to errupt the Tibetans were taking pressure off the California continental plates. We saved San Francisco.

I had gone to several family physicians about my physical problems of which dioxin poisining seemed to be the cause and I thought it was also causing my adjustment problems but the family doctors never realized what was happening to me and I stopped going to them and instead thought this Tibetan buddhist lama would be able to help me, because I did realize that something was wrong.

I was losing contact with reality gradually and stayed in abject poverty and I was miserable. I remember I bought a WW 2 rifle to please the WW 2 veteran and I would sit in my basement room with the barrel in my mouth and wonder if I should pull the trigger. I started to think Tashi Namjal was evil because he was celibate and I got messages from Beatle songs which I thought were from the Marharishi Mahesh Yogi to run away and that's what I did. I thought there was a war going on between two groups, both with supernatural powers, that would decide the fate of humanity. I called one the Sexuals and one the Anti-sexuals, because these powers came from sexuality.

I forget some of my life out west. I do remember being very miserable and very alone, identifying with Milarepa who is a Tibetan saint of sorts. The Tantric tradition, which is very interesting, has its roots in India. In the ninth century these supernormal powers were close to becoming a part of society. Tibetan buddhism incorporates a celibate tantricism in its teachings which has survived I think because it is also very religious. I was entranced by the erotic temples in India like Konarak and determined to become a tantric and help the world rediscover the supernormal powers of the mind in sexuality.

In Toronto I managed to get a job changing lightbulbs at a large department store. I ran away twice, to England and Jamaica expecting to be welcomed personally by the Maharishi. When a terrorist bomb blew up a plane over Lockerbie Scotland I thought it was an attempt on my life, which prompted me to fly immediately to the Maharishi in England but he wasn't there and I came back the same weekend. I saw a movie called "Oedipus Rex" directed by Passolini and immediately flew to Jamaica expecting to meet the Maharishi. I was looking for Strawberry Fields mentioned in the Beatles song and there are two in Jamaica. It was a memorable trip. I ran out of money after one week and mostly learned the importance of money.

I was just a pawn in a secret war. I didn't have any friends, any lovers, and very little contact with my parents between 1980 and 1990. My parents had moved to the States while I was in Victoria and I never told anyone what was happening. I lived in a cockroach infested rooming house never even realizing that Diazinon will eliminate cockroaches. I had a strong sense of mission to help humanity instead of myself and in my poverty I believed the cause of suffering in the world was overpopulation. My solution was to hybridize the AIDS virus with the common cold and eliminate 3–4 billion people.

I got a lot of messages from favorite Rock and Roll songs, from movies, cartoons and library books. The library was my special friend who could show me what I needed to know by having me open and read exactly the information I was looking for. Someone was leading me to the books I needed and that was too much for humans to be capable of. I started to believe I was in contact with aliens from outer space. At first there were two kinds. I learned humanity was going to become extinct from a nuclear holocaust that would break up the continental plates. The oceans would evaporate with all the molten lava and I was going to live in a box out in space with a woman the aliens had been breeding since life started on this planet. She had dark blue skin like the Hindu god Krishna and we were going to have children who would be turquoise in colour. We were going to be the only survivors of Armageddon and we would propagate the species. Only girls would be born as identical twins and they would be able to impregnate each other from a single drop on their funny long noses. I would be the last surviving male although I would only live a thousand years.

I believed that to be my destiny completely and got a lot of messages everywhere I went. I heard voices several times but mostly I experienced telepathy. I had what are called "ideas of reference" where things are thought to have a particular meaning just for you. For example, a license plate on the street could be an important and appropriate message for me from the aliens. By the end my fate had changed a bit. I was going to become an alien and have eternal life and be capable of time travel and my companion was going to be a part time anthropolgy professor at the University of Toronto. Sexuality was as important as intelligence to the aliens and they had evolved beyond the use of machinery to doing everything with their mind. I thought they were turning on my nervous system with experiences of pain so that every neuron was active, so that I would be able to experience greater pleasure as an alien. I asked them once if a machine might not make the process less painful and I remember them laughing, saying "Machines…Ian, we don't have any machines."

My delusions changed as the aliens instructed me on the real nature of reality. Three things happened as my contact with reality became very tenuous. I got in trouble with the law, I became alcoholic, and I lost my job.

One night after convincing the aliens to transfer my mind to another body I got mad at the aliens, and started breaking windows in the rooming house I was living in. The police came, subdued me and I spent a couple of nights in jail. The judge realized I was a psychiatric case because I carried a pocketknife to defend myself against homosexuals. The world's most powerful man was a homosexual and he was trying to make me a homosexual. By then the Maharishi was my second worst enemy. I believed they both knew about the end of the world and my destiny with the aliens and they wanted to take my place. I didn't mention that in court though.

Nobody asked why I did what I did. I got three years probation with the condition that I see a psychiatrist for those three years. Psychiatrists are only human though, while I was almost alien and they wouldn't have understood what was happening so I never told them anything. I went to my appointments to stay out of jail.

Jail was such a shock to me. I was so mad at the aliens after that experience I tried to force them to give me a new body by killing the body I was in. I bought several bottles of vodka and guzzled them like water until I passed out knowing that people overdose and die from alcohol. I got pneumonia but lived and decided that the aliens wouldn't let me die, only experience pain until it was time for me to go.

Although I didn't drink anything for awhile I eventually started to drink and heavily because I could afford it. You need $11 an hour to become an alcoholic. Originally I drank for the hops which I thought were medication for celibacy. My behaviour became more and more bizarre and I was fired from my job. I went from unemployment insurance to Welfare, brewing my own beer in plastic pails and eating in soup kitchens. I thought I was going to become an alien when I turned 37 because I saw a book written by the ancient seer Nostradamus entitled 3791. I thought that since he could see the future he would realize I was not capable of understanding the book and that all I would need to know could be explained in the title. I turned 37 in 1991 a year after moving to Guelph but I'm still here unfortunately.

I experienced many extreme emotions when I was psychotic with positive symptoms. In fact its a wonder I didn't come into contact with the police before I did. I can say that I never harmed anyone but I realize I came very close, although I experienced more fear than anything else. I am by nature a gentle person who has never fought with anyone. Family members I have met in Guelph have usually had some experience of verbal abuse or physical assault from their ill relative before they were treated. I remember I thought I was dying from celibacy and I hated women for a couple years even though I went through adolescence with only feminist friends and was convinced women were the superior sex. Schizophrenia can force you to feel and do things that are not in character for you. Dr. E Fuller Torrey says violence in schizophrenia is predicted by three factors,

a previous history of violence,
substance abuse,
not on medication

    I would destroy my own possesions first like my guitar without hav-ing much choice. I shied away from people. I remember sitting on the ledge of a window on the sixth floor wanting to jump but knowing that the aliens would have an open truck loaded with mattresses come by just as I jumped and when I actually saw such a truck weeks later it only confirmed my conclusions.

    I didn't win the lottery though after I lost my job and the people in my rooming house started mainlining heroin in the living room. I was desperately poor by that point expecting to become homeless and sleep on a hot air vent and I couldn't believe that was necessary in becoming an alien. I was experiencing quite a few blackouts from the drinking I was doing and getting scared of alcohol. I kept waking up in strange places. One fellow in the rooming house had attacked me with a chain such that I needed stitches above my eye. I was too disorganized and too poor to find another place to live. My mind seemed to be falling apart into the left brain, me, and a right brain I hardly knew who was in tremendous pain and very demanding, and a dinosaur or core brain, very powerful and very angry at me. I agreed to go to the Homewood Health Centre in Guelph to be treated for alcoholism. Going into hos-pital was the easy way to get out of a situation that was very frighten-ing. That was at the end of my three year probationary period.

    As I sobered up my delusions faded a lot and I realized I had no con-crete proof of aliens or my imaginary wife. I also realized I couldn't put my faith in aliens to take care of me. I moved into a basement room in Guelph and started a maintenance dose of antipsychotics. The year was 1990. It took several years to completely believe and understand that I had schizophrenia though. I was sure I had been misdiagnosed, and I would much rather have had bipolar disorder so I could compare myself to various famous people. I wanted to go off medication but the psychiatrists were very firm about that. Medication didn't seem to have any effect so there was no reason not to take it. It kept my psychiatrist happy.

I was very depressed for several years and very lethargic. I didn't accomplish very much and was quite anxious. I lived in basement rooms, had no friends and little contact with anyone. At that time I was seeing a psychiatrist at the Community Mental Health Clinic once a month or so. I don't think my period of depression could have been avoided. Antidepressants didn't help which suggests I didn't have an actual depression. I was very anxious having nothing to do and no one to do it with and had very low self esteem. My mood eventually improved a bit and I made a couple of friends and became more active. I started to do a little volunteer work and I eventually met Rosemary and courted her. I started to work for some extra cash, delivering flyers and then the local newspaper. Rosemary and I moved into the apartment building where I delivered newspapers. We shared a two bedroom apartment for 16 months until the Provincial government chnaged the rules on cohabitation and it became too expensive.

The quality of my life has been improving a little each year for the last ten years and I can't complain too much but every once in awhile I really feel the losses I am enduring. Life is a series of opportunities as you grow older, and I missed all of them. It is only in the past couple of years that I can say that I have been able to accomplish anything productive. Before that I was pretty unhappy and didn't feel very good about myself.

My friend Susan says there are two kinds of people. You get on a plane that is supposed to go to Hawaii and instead the plane lands in Siberia. Susan prefers to use Arizona as the alternate destination. You can either learn to enjoy Siberia or forever feel bitter that you didn't land in Hawaii. Lately Siberia has been fairly pleasant. My life does seem a bit "empty" compared to ordinary peoples lives. I also have a lot of unpleasant memories in which I've done things I now regret. Its difficult to know how much I'm responsible for and how much schizophrenia is responsible for. I think its important for me to focus on enjoying life as much as I can and not dwell on the past.

I went to an international conference on Schizophrenia in 1996, sponsored by Eli Lilly. I was mistakenly booked at the hotel as Dr. Chovil and the next day at the conference in my sports coat and dress shirt I was just another psychiatrist and it felt pretty neat. This was the life I should have had. But the first keynote address by Dr. Weinberger, world reknown researcher in schizophrenia, compared finding the cause of schizophrenia to finding the cause of the TWA flight explosion that was in the news at that time. There was no evidence that it was a bomb. Finding out what happened when all you have are the twisted pieces of metal scattered along the ocean floor was causing difficulties. Over the three day conference I became very depressed realizing how appropriate that image was for me. I could empathise with the psychiatrists who were looking at their patient in front of them and asking themselves "why doesn't this person have the same lifestyle that I enjoy?".

There is hope on the horizon in the new atypicals and early diagnosis, coupled with relapse prevention, and schizophrenia seems to be attracting much more public interest and compassion. There is so much research underway on schizophrenia it's difficult to keep up with it.

Ian's recovery:

My Recovery—so far

People have asked me to write about my recovery, and my first response is "what recovery?". My second is that I mostly want to educate people about schizophrenia. I use the word "recovery" like I use the word "love". If I ever feel it you'll be the first to know. On the other hand though, I've come a long way in the ten years that I've been taking my medication. I was invited to meet and chat with Her Honour, Hillary Weston, Lieutenant Governor of Ontario. I was invited to meet and chat with the Premier of Ontario, Mike Harris at a press conference during the last election. Our local MPP Brenda Elliott and I have met several times, and she knows me well. I've been quoted in about two dozen newspapers in the past few years, several times on the front page, and my experiences featured in a half dozen of them. I've appeared on three 6 o'clock television news reports and recently, the CBC National news. I won the Courage to Come Back Award from the Clarke Institute Foundation and the Flag of Hope Award from the Schizophrenia Society of Canada in 1998. The Schizophrenia Bulletin, which is probably the leading journal in schizophrenia, recently published my First Person Account. More locally I was recently presented with a Mayor's Award of Excellence in Guelph. There are four given out each year. I think it says more about what a great place Guelph is, where the stigma of mental illness is so minimal they are willing to present an award to someone with schizophrenia, arguably the most disabling and stigmatized of all the mental illnesses.

I have a modest one bedroom I really enjoy, and I work in a half time staff position at Homewood Health Centre. I'm still leading a fairly solitary life, but the Homewood, my volunteer work, and my nascent computer skills bring me into almost daily contact with a wide variety of people. Over the last four years I've met a lot of people. My "recovery" created a new problem for me, remembering people's names.

I would say I actually have a fairly interesting life, such as it is, which is in sharp contrast to how I felt when I first started on medication. Those first few years were horrible, especially when I realized I wasn't going to return to graduate school and pick up where I left off in 1978. How would I meet women if not at university? I didn't see any alternatives to school except a very marginal and solitary life on the fringes of society. I would be quote unquote, "a loser". With an invisible disability, and one the public knew very little about, I didn't expect to be treated very well. But it was pretty obvious I would never be able to complete any university.

The Toronto consumer/survivor movement has a slogan: "a home, a job, and a friend". That's what they want. With my history, I couldn't really imagine the job part. I'd rather collect disability benefits than wash dishes in some restaurant. In fact I've never really been employed since I graduated from university, at least never in a job I enjoyed.

Ironically much of the "recovery" I'm having has come about because I love the work I am doing. Some of it is volunteer and some of it is paid. I volunteered and worked in the mental health field where people did treat me with considerable respect, although I had to earn it more often than not. Some people went way out of their way to accommodate me.

After a number of years on medication, both my case manager and psychiatrist suggested I volunteer somewhere. I was complaining to one that I had no money, and to the other that I had no girlfriend. So I tried volunteering without much success. Even the minimal requirement of showing up somewhere when I said I would was too much for me. I was just about to give up on Maclean Hunter Community television, when I took part in one of a four part series on mental illness. I proposed a ten part series on the mental health system to the station programmer, and detailed each episode of confirmed guests. Suddenly I was a producer, but when the taping was finished I quit that volunteer job. About then I started part time paid work delivering flyers and then newspapers. I had to swallow my pride to mix with ten year olds delivering the daily paper, and it's quite a challenge really, because you deliver them every day, and every day before 5 PM, except weekends when it's 9 am. I liked it but was a little embarrassed collecting from customers. It also became fashionable to have people with a psychiatric diagnosis sit on various committees and boards, and I could handle an hour at a time with only a little difficulty.

My friends, and I, most of whom had schizophrenia and were unemployed, found ordinary people were so different, not by nature, but by their different lifestyle. They had careers, families, cars, children, new clothes. We lived a very different life with our basement room and second hand clothes, watching the cars drive by as we walked to where ever we were going. Ordinary people marched to a different drum beat, a very different drum beat. It was difficult to even have a conversation with them. Some of my friends felt uncomfortable with ordinary people and would turn down any invitations that involved socializing with them.

Slowly I am becoming, for lack of a better word, "reintegrated". I became more and more capable of socializing with ordinary people. That's not to say I don't have a long way to go, it's just that I can interact with people better, professionally more than socially, but that may just be my personality. It's become very difficult for anyone to guess I have schizophrenia, even professionals. I also started to become productive in a way that was meaningful for me. Even with the paper route, I could look back to an accomplishment that I had earned money from, and I could start spending that money on whatever was important to me, like new clothes and computer stuff. I've been fairly successful in most of the projects I've undertaken at the Homewood, some more than others. I get a lot of positive feedback and support, particularly from family members. The Homewood gives me a pretty free hand in when and where I work and I track my own hours.

I courted Rosemary three years ago, and we lived together for a year and a half. We didn't actually have very much in common. We got to know each other inside out though and she is still my best friend. I think I'm about fourth on her list, after her mother, sister, and her new Shipoo puppy. Recently I had major surgery for Crohn's disease, which involves taking out sections of the large and small intestine. The pathology report found cancerous cells in that section of intestine and suddenly my mortality became very much more real. I was off work for eight weeks, amazed by the get well cards and flower arrangements coming to my door. I was really touched actually.

My barometer of recovery has always been annual earned income and long term romantic relationships. I had been supplementing my disability benefits with part time work for the last six years. In my new position at the Homewood I'm making too much to stay on disability benefits. I'm a bit worried about that because this job is very unique and the only one I could do. If it ends, for some reason, there is no other position I could apply for.

Family members can't believe how well I've recovered from schizophrenia and I get chided for seeing the glass as half empty instead of half full. The past is half empty, future promises to be half full. But recovered I'm not, and to be honest I feel like a fish out of water most of the time.

Personal Story III: DR. ROSEMARY RODGERS

The army has done a lot to people—both good and bad. Not only physically…but mentally. I remember in my book "Musings of a Mad Madam" talking about those people that were in they army that were involuntarily committed to the mental institution that I was in. I remembered often how they came in (usually loudly and restrained) and how they left (always doped up and docile as the commanding officer toted them away). I spoke with one fellow patient about the army and she told me how they gave her all these drugs that made her violent…and never to trust the army. The other 5 people that were in the same boat as she agreed. They all stated how the army shoved them into psychiatrists offices-gave them hasty diagnoses and forced 'therapeutic' drugs down their throats that were anything but. Dr. Rosemary Rodgers story reminds me of this. Here are excerpts from her story: Her story is in letter format: Dr. Rodgers was diagnosed as a paranoid schizophrenic back when she was in the army in the early 70's. She has a bevy of letters and documentation and is fighting a battle against the U.S. Army against her unfair treatment. Here are snippets from her letters from her website: **www.tripping.org**

Does external stress (eg. noise) equal paranoid schizophrenia?

The U.S. Army claims it does. The Army uses manmade noise such as tapping or pen-clicking as an aversive stimulus to produce stress. Noise is tasteless, odorless, invisible, intangible, and leaves no trace. It is an assault without touch.

Chronic noise assaults the amygdala and the hippocampus in the limbic system of the brain causing anxiety, aggression, memory loss, and cognitive impairment.

Cognitive impairment and difficulty dealing with stress are features of schizophrenia. Schizophrenia is a functional psychiatric disorder. This means there is no radiology study or blood test to diagnose schizophrenia. It is not an organic disease with clearcut pathological features.

Psychiatrists diagnose schizophrenia by a set of criteria listed in the Diagnostic and Statistical Manual of Mental Disorders (DSMIV). Cardinal symptoms of schizophrenia include delusions and hallucinations (hearing voices and seeing unreal images).

Letter 2:

The first thing I remember learning in my freshman lectures at Northwestern University Medical School was "*primum non nocere*"—first do no harm. Physicians at Northwestern, the Mayo Clinic, and in the Army have surely broken this rule with regard to me.

The worst thing you can do to a person short of killing him is to disable him. The army has tried to disable me through manmade noise harassment.

When I wrote to Congressman Jerry Weller about this harrassment, he wrote to Tripler Army Medical Center in Honolulu where I was stationed from October, 1979 till November, 1981. The Commander of Tripler, Brigadier General James E. Hastings answered Mr. Weller, "Unfortunately, we are unable to respond to this inquiry. Dr. Rodgers left Tripler almost 15 years ago and our records of her psychiatric treatment or alleged harassment are no longer on file."

Letter 3:

In the novel *Coma* Robin Cook's heroine is a female medical student who discovers a plot led by the Chief of Surgery at her medical school to kill surgery patients and sell their organs for transplant. When the surgeon learns she knows, he attempts to kill her.

I wonder how many female physicians have died needlessly at Northwestern University Medical School. The female death rate there seems very high to me. I think someone should investigate it.

Dr. Loyal Davis, a neurosurgeon and Ronald Reagan's father-in-law, was Chief of Surgery at Passavant Hospital, an affiliate of Northwestern Medical School, for many years. I visited him in April, 1981 at his home in Phoenix, Arizona where he was living in retirement. He had learned earlier the same day I visited him that he had metastatic cancer. When I arrived at his house, he had a large bandage on his left ear. His demented wife was living with him. They had a full-time live-in nurse staying at their home.

I had met Dr. Davis when I was a junior medical student on the Passavant surgical service. When I made rounds with him, he gave me his neurological kit to carry for him. Dr. Davis had always had a mean, nasty reputation among Northwestern medical students. They retaliated by telling indigent unmarried women of color to name their newborn infants Loyal Davis. In her autobiography *Nancy*, Nancy Reagan likens her stepfather Loyal Davis to Iago.

When I complained to Dr. Davis of the harassment I was experiencing at Tripler Army Medical Center in Honolulu, he told me I was "paranoid." He said women don't belong in the Army. He told me to go work in a small town, but that I wouldn't like that any better. He had worked in Galesburg, Illinois after medical school before his surgical training. He didn't like Galesburg.

When I returned to duty at Tripler after my visit to see Dr. Davis, the harassment escalated. Instead of just whistling and crude verbal noises, I was subjected to finger drumming, pen clicking, and overflights of noisy, unmarked twin engine planes every time I entered and exited Tripler Hospital.

Letter 5:

There have been many books, plays, and films dealing with psychiatric issues, but there are three I'd like to discuss with reference to my plight. First, of course, is the novel *One Flew Over the Cuckoo's Nest* by Ken Kesey. In his book Kesey shows how power can be abused by psychiatric physicians and nurses (Nurse Ratched). In fact, their abuse of power led to the rebel hero McMurphy's death.

Next is the classic film *Gaslight* starring Ingrid Bergman and Charles Boyer. This movie is so well known that the word "gaslight" has become an English verb. The character Boyer plays tries to drive Bergman's character mad. Now the U. S. Army is trying to gaslight me. It's a very old trick.

The last work I'd like to discuss is the play *Harvey* by Mary Chase. This is my favorite because it's a comedy, but also very pertinent to my situation. The main character in this play Elwood P. Dowd has an imaginary friend who is a big white rabbit named Harvey. Mr. Dowd is a pleasant, harmless man, but his sister tries to commit him to a private asylum. The staff of the asylum are really the dysfunctional people in the play. Fortunately, in the end Mr. Dowd eludes the asylum staff and returns home to live with his family and Harvey, the rabbit.

I hope my life doesn't end like McMurphy's. I would like to expose the bad people like Charles Boyer's character in *Gaslight* who are tormenting me and return to a nice life like Elwood P. Dowd did. Hopefully, I won't even need a friend like Harvey.

Letter 6:

Happy New Year! 1 had planned to write about the power of the U.S. military, but I'll postpone that subject until next time. Instead 1 like to discuss the hit movie *Patch Adams* which I just saw over Christmas.

I enjoyed this new film staring Robin Williams. It is a typical Hollywood make-you-feel-good movie. When the film ended, I felt good, but later I reflected on the movie's subplot of the female medical student. and 1 had second thoughts.

This movie is about a fellow *Patch Adams* who goes to medical school because he wants to help people, not just make money. He is a likable guy who knows how to make people laugh and feel comfortable. So far, so good. But the female medical student in this story has a weak personality and a history of continuing abuse by men, gets mediocre grades, and ends up being murdered by a psychotic.

I gather from this story that women doctors are weak and expendable. There are few books or films that portray women doctors as strong characters or heroines. A notable exception was the series CBS aired for several seasons with Jane Seymour as an American frontier doctor.

Even with medical school classes now roughly half and half men and women, women still get the short straw. Women continue to enter less prestigious specialties like pediatrics, internal medicine, and psychiatry while men predominate in surgery.

In 1998, a female physician was elected for the first time as President of the American Medical Association (AMA), but I question whether her election was orchestrated to entice more women to join the falling ranks of the AMA membership. The new executive director of the AMA holds a permanent position, has a military background, and is a man. He actually wields the real power at the AMA, not the President who is a figurehead.

I do not know what it will take for women to obtain equal power and prestige with men in medicine. Women have impediments to career advancement such as childbirth, child-rearing, and housework. Women, as a whole, are not as aggressive as men. Women generally do not have access to the predominately male networks at the major medical clinics, universities, and government organizations. Women lack role models and mentors.

Using myself as an example, I was the only female in the Thoracic Department at the Mayo Clinic between 1974 and 1976. There were about twelve other male fellows in training and twenty-five consultants. I felt isolated and trapped. The Mayo Clinic used me as a workhorse and gave me no benefits in retum. The Clinic definitely discouraged my attempts to perform research. Anything I got out of the Mayo Clinic experience was due purely to my own efforts. Although I received very high scores on the American Board of Internal Medicine Pulmonary exam in 1976, I barely received one letter of congratulations from the men at the Mayo Clinic.

If you want to see a good movie. go see *Patch Adams*. But remember to question the depiction of the female medical student in the this film.

Letter 7:

With the New Year here and the millenium due next year, 1 think it is appropriate to discuss the current power of the U.S. military. Since the dissolution of the Soviet Union there is only one superpower left: the United States. The U.S. Army is the strongest Army in the world. It is unopposed. It has unlimited economic resources.

1 feel the U.S. Army is too powerful. Power corrupts and absolute power corrupts absolutely. The U.S. Army is getting away with murder. It has both biological and chemical weapons. It opposes the ban on land mines. It feels that it is the policeman of the world. It intervenes in the war in Bosnia and attacks Iraq when lraq does not comply with its demands.

What is there to check the power of the U.S. military establishment? It is difficult to attack something that is so well fortified. Long ago

Dwight Eisenhower warned us against the military-industrial complex, and he was a general. Congress continues to appropriate money for the military, but rarely investigates it. I am sure there are plenty of things more important to investigate in the military than in the Clinton presidency.

The Republican Party has always had a cozy relationship with the military. I wouldn't be surprised if some generals were behind the attacks on Clinton because they resent that Clinton dodged the draft during the Viet Nam War.

The U.S. Army is harassing and trying to kill me. I was one of their own officers. Whenever I try to have congressmen and senators investigate my predicament, the Army stonewalls.

Perhaps in the future European countries will unite militarily as they have economically (the Euro). A European army could counterbalance the American Army. After all, Europeans are old hands at war. They have fought wars far longer than Americans have.

References

Aberg-Wistedt, A., Cressell, T., Lidberg, Y., & Liljenberg, B. (1995). Two-year outcome of team-based intensive case management for patients with schizophrenia. Psychiatric Services, 46(12), 1263–1266.

"African Americans." (2001). The Department of Arkansas Heritage. Retrieved July 10, 2001 from the World Wide Web at **<http://www.arkansasheritage.com/peoplestories/africanamerican/main.html>**.

Airhihenbuwa C.O., Kumanyika S., Agurs T.D., Lowe A., Saunders D., & Morssink C.B. (1996, September). Cultural aspects of African American eating patterns. Ethnic Health, 1(3), 245–60.

Alaghband-Rad, J.; Hamburger, S.D.; Giedd, J.N., et al. (1997). Childhood-onset schizophrenia: biological markets in relation to clinical characteristics. American Journal Psychiatry, 154 (1), 64–68.

American Psychiatric Association (APA) (1997). Practice guideline for the treatment of patients with schizophrenia. American Journal Psychiatry, 154 (4 Supplement), 1–54.

American Psychiatric Association (APA) (1997). Practice guideline for the treatment of patients with schizophrenia. American Journal Psychiatry, 154 (4 Supplement), 1–54.

American Psychiatric Association. (1986). Diagnostic and Statistical Manual of Mental Disorders. Washington, D.C.: APA.

American Psychiatric Association. <u>Diagnostic And Statistical Manual Of Mental Disorders.</u> 4th Ed., 285–286. Washington, DC: Author, 1994.

American Psychiatric Association. (1994). <u>Diagnostic and statistical manual of mental disorders, DSM-IV.</u> Washington: American Psychiatric Association.

American Psychiatric Association (APA) (1997). Practice guideline for the treatment of patients with schizophrenia. <u>American Journal Psychiatry</u>, 154 (4 Supplement), 1–54.

Aritei, S. (1955). Interpretation of Schizophrenia. New York: R. Brunner.

Axelson M.L. (1986). The impact of culture on food-related behavior. <u>Annual Review of Nutrition, 6</u>, 345–363.

Basiotis, P.P, Lino, M., & Anand, R.S. (1998). Report card on the diet quality of African Americans. <u>Family Economic and Nutrition Review, 11</u>(3), 61–63.

Beeber, A. R. (1991). Psychotherapy with Schizophrenics in Team Groups: A Systems Model. <u>American Journal of Psychotherapy, 45,</u> 78–87.

Bender, K. J. (1998). Dietary Fatty Acids Essential for Mental Health. <u>Psychiatric Times, 16.</u>

Beardsley, T. (1997). Matter Over Mind: Do Viruses Cause Severe Mental Illness? Scientific American, 1–2.

Beck, A.T. (1967). Depression: Clinical, Theoretical and experimental. New York: Harper & Row.

Bielanska, A., Cechnicki, A., & Budzyna-Dawidowski, P.. (1991). Drama therapy as a means of rehabilitation for schizophrenic patients. American Journal of Psychotherapy, 45(4), 566–575.

Brown, S., Birtwistle, J., Roe, L., & Thompson, C. (1999). The unhealthy lifestyle of people with schizophrenia. Psychological Medicine, 29, 697–701.

Carpenter, W. T., Jr., & Buchanan, R. W. (1994, 10 March). New England Journal of Medicine, 330, 681–690.

Cognitive help for schizophrenia. (1992, 11 April). Science News, 141(15), 239.

Carter, M. & Flesher, S. (1995). The neurosociology of schizophrenia: vulnerability and functional disability. Psychiatry, 58 (August), 209–224.

Carter, M. & Flesher, S. (1995). The neurosociology of schizophrenia: vulnerability and functional disability. Psychiatry, 58 (August), 209–224.

Chu, C., & Sallach, H. (1985). Differences in psychopathology among black and white schizophrenics. International Journal of Social Psychiatry, 31(4), 252–257.

Cohen, S.M., Allen, M.G., Pollini, W., & Hrtibec, Z. (1972). Relationship of schizo-affective Psychosis To Manic Depression And Schizophrenia. Archives of General Psychiatry, 26(6), 539–546.

Coleman, D., & Baker, F. (1994). Misdiagnosis of Schizophrenia in Older, Black veterans. Journal of Nervous and Mental Disease, 182(9), 527–528. Chang, E.C. (1996). Cultural Differences in Optimism, Pessimism, and Coping. Journal of Counseling Psychology, 44(1), 113–123.

Coleman, J.C. (1989). Abnormal Psychology and Modern Life. Evanston, IL: Scott, Foresman and Co.

Conte, H. R. (1994). Review of Research in Supportive Psychotherapy: An Update. American Journal of Psychotherapy, 48, 494–505.

Davison G.C., & Neale, J.M. (1986). Abnormal Psychology. New York: John Wiley and Sons.

Dietz, P. (1998). Perspective On Mental Illness. Los Angeles Times. Jan. 25, 1–3.

Dilts, R., Hallbom, T., & Smith, S. (1993). Beliefs: Pathways to health & well-being. Portland, Oregon: Metamorphous Press.

Dohan F.C. (1969). Schizophrenia: possible relationship to cereal grains and coeliac disease. In: S. Sanker (Ed.), Schizophrenia Current Concepts and Research, (539–551). Hicksville, NY: PJD Publications.

Dohan, F.C., Harper, E.H., Clark, M.H., Rodrigue, R.B., & Zigas, V. (1984). Is schizophrenia rare if grain is rare. Biological Psychiatry, 19(3), 385–398.

Eagles, John M. (1991). Is schizophrenia disappearing? British Journal of Psychiatry, 158, 834–835.

Fabrega, H., Mezzich, J., & Ulrich, R. (1966). Black-White Differences In Psychopathology In An Urban Psychiatric Population. Comprehensive Psychiatry 29(3), 265–297.

Fallon, S. & Enig, M. G. (1999). Tripping Lightly Down the Prostaglandin Pathways. Price-Pottenger Nutrition Foundation.

Fenton, W. S., Hibbein, J., & Knable, M. (1999). Essential Fatty Acids, Lipid Membrane Abnormalities, and the Diagnosis and

Treatment of Schizophrenia. Society of Biological Psychiatry, 47,
Fine, R. (1989). A History of Psychoanalysis. New York: Columbia University Press.

Flaskerud, J., & Eu, L. (1992). Relationship Of Ethnicity To Psychiatric Diagnosis. Journal of Nervous and Mental Disease, 180(5), 296–303.

Fullilove, M. (1986). Healing the Lineage. American Journal of Social Psychiatry, 6(1), 3–5. 8–21.

Garety, P. A., Kuipers, L., Fowler, D., & Chamberlain, F. (1994, September). Cognitive-behavior therapy for drug-resistant psychosis. British Journal of medical Psychology, 67(3), 259–271.

Garfield, S.L. & Bergin, A.E. (1990). Handbook of Psychotherapy and Behavior Change. New York: John Wiley and Sons.

Gottesman I, & Shields J. (1972). Schizophrenia and Genetics: A Twin Study Vantage Point. New York: Academic Press.

Gruenberg, A. M., Kendler, K. S., & Tsuang, M. T. (1985). Reliability and concordance in the subtyping of schizophrenia. American Journal of Psychiatry, 142, 1355–1358.

Gur, R.E.; Petty, R.G.; Turetsky, B.E., Gur, R.C. (1996). Schizophrenia throughout life: sex differences in severity and profile of symptoms. Schizophrenia Research, 21, 1–12.

Gur, R.E.; Petty, R.G.; Turetsky, B.E., Gur, R.C. (1996). Schizophrenia throughout life: sex differences in severity and profile of symptoms. Schizophrenia Research, 21, 1–12.

Gur, R.E.; Petty, R.G.; Turetsky, B.E., Gur, R.C. (1996). Schizophrenia throughout life: sex differences in severity and profile of symptoms. Schizophrenia Research, 21, 1–12.

Halford, W. K. (1994). Behavior therapy and schizophrenia. Behavior Change, 11(4), 195–199.

Hanes, K.R.; Andrewes, D.G.; Pantelis, C.; & Chiu, E. (1996). Subcortical dysfunction in schizophrenia: a comparison with Parkinson's disease and Huntington's disease. Schizophrenia Research, 19, 121–128.

Harvard University. (2001). The Psychosocial Treatment of Schizophrenia—Part I. Harvard Mental Health Letter, 18, 1–5.

Hillbrand, M., Spitz, R. T., & VandenBos, G. R. (1997). Investigating the Role of Lipids in Mood, Aggression, and Schizophrenia. Psychiatric Services, 48, 875–876.

Hodel, B., & Brenner, H.D. (1997). A new development in integrated psychological therapy for schizophrenia patients. In H.D. Brenner, W. Boker, & R. Genner, Eds., Towards a Comprehensive Therapy for Schizophrenia. Gottingen, Germany: Hogrefe & Huber, 118–134.

Holzman, P.S. (1996). On the trail of the genetics and pathophysiology of schizophrenia. Psychiatry, 59 (May), 117–127.

Honig, A. M. (1991). Psychotherapy with Command Hallucinations in Chronic Schizophrenia: The Use of Action Techniques Within a Surrogate Family Setting. Journal of Group Psychotherapy, 44, 3–19.

Horrobin, D. F., Manku, M. S., Morse-Fisher, N. Vaddadi, K. S., Courtney, P., Iain, A., Glen, M., Glen, E., Spellman, M., & Bates, C. (1989). Essential Fatty Acids in Plasma Phospholipids in Schizophrenics. Society of Biological Psychiatry, 25, 562–568.

Horrobin, D. F., Hanku, M. S., Hillman, H., Iain, A. & Glen, M. (1991). Fatty Acid Levels in the Brains of Schizophrenics and Normal Controls. Society of Biological Psychiatry, 30, 795–805.

Horrobin, D. F. (1999). Interactions Between Lipid Metabolism and Schizophrenia: The Biochemical Changes Which May Have Made Us Human. Lipids, 34, 5255.

Hunt, L. (1996). "The Simple Facts On Split Brain Disorder." Independent. Jan. 16, 1–3.

Jackson, D. D. (1964). Myths of Madness. Macmillian Company, New York.

Johnstone, E. C. (1993, 27 February). Schizophrenia: Problems in clinical practice. Lancet, 341, 536–538.

Jones, B., & Gray, B. (1966). Problems in diagnosing schizophrenia and affective disorders among blacks. Hospital and Community Psychiatry, 37(1), 61–65.

Joy, C. B., Mumby-Croft, R., & Joy, L. A. (2000). Polyunsaturated Fatty Acid (Fish or Evening Primrose Oil) for Schizophrenia (Cochrane Review). In: The Cochrane Library, 3. Oxford: Update Software.

Jung, C. G. (1956). Two Essays on Analytical Psychology, Translated by R.F.C. Hull. New York: The World Publishing Company.

Kaiya, H., Horrobin, D. F., Manku, M. S., & Fisher, N. M. (1991). Essential and Other Fatty Acids in Plasma in Schizophrenics and Normal Individuals from Japan. Society of Biological Psychiatry, 30, 357–362.

Kaplan, H. I., & Sadock, B. J. (1991). Comprehensive Textbook of Psychiatry/V, Vol. 2, (5th ed.). Baltimore: The Williams & Wilkins Co.

Karlsson, J. L. (1966). The Biological Basis of Schizophrenia. Springfield, Illinois: Lcharles C. Thomas.

Kane, J. M. (1996). Schizophrenia. New England Journal of Medicine, 334, 34–41.

Kates, J. & Rockland, L. H. (1994). Supportive Psychotherapy of the Schizophrenic Patient. American Journal of Psychotherapy, 48, 543–562.

Kendler, K.S.; MacLean, C.J.; O'Neill, A.; Burke, J., et al (1996). Evidence for a schizophrenia vulnerability locus on chromosome 8p in the Irish study of high-density schizophrenia families. American Journal of Psychiatry, 153 (12), 1534–1540.

Kendler K.S. (1983). Overview: A current perspective on twin studies of schizophrenia. American Journal of Psychiatry, 140, 1413–1425.

Kendler K.S., & Diehl S.R. (1993). The genetics of schizophrenia: A current, genetic-epidemiologic perspective. Schizophrenia Bulletin, 19, 261–285.

Kendler, K.S.; MacLean, C.J.; O'Neill, A.; Burke, J., et al (1996). Evidence for a schizophrenia vulnerability locus on chromosome 8p in the Irish study of high-density schizophrenia families. American Journal of Psychiatry, 153 (12), 1534–1540.

Kendler, K. S., Spitzer, R. L., & Williams, J. B. W. (1989). Psychotic disorders in DSM-III-R. American Journal of Psychiatry, 146(8), 953–962.

Kittler P.G. & Sucher K. A (1989). Food and Culture in America. A Nutrition Handbook, New York: Van Nostrand.

Kwon J.S., McCarley R.W., Hirayasu Y., Anderson J.E., Fischer I.A., Kikinis R., Jolesz F.A., & Shenton M.E. (1999). Left planum temporale volume reduction in schizophrenia. Archives of General Psychiatry, 56, 142–148.

Laing, R. D. & Esterton, A. (1965). Sanity, Madness, and the Family. New York: Basic Books.

Larsen, T.K. & Opjordsmoen, S. (1996). Early identification and treatment of schizophrenia: conceptual and ethical considerations. Psychiatry, 59 (Winter), 371–380.

Larsen, T.K. & Opjordsmoen, S. (1996). Early identification and treatment of schizophrenia: conceptual and ethical considerations. Psychiatry, 59 (Winter), 371–380.

Lawson, W., Hepler, N., Holladay, J., & Cuffel, B. (1994). Race a factor in inpatient and outpatient admissions and diagnosis. Hospital and Community Psychiatry, 45(1), 72–74.

Lefley, H.P. (1997). The consumer recovery vision: will it alleviate family burden? American Journal of Orthopsychiatry, 67 (2), 210–219.

Le Fevre, P.D. (2001). Improving the physical health of patients with schizophrenia: therapeutic nihilism or realism? Scottish Medical Journal, 46, 11–13.

Lehman, A.F. (1995). Vocational rehabilitation in schizophrenia. Schizophrenia Bulletin, 21 (4), 645–656.

Leszek, J., Inglot, A. D., Cantell, K., & Wasik, A. (1991). Natural human leukocyte interferon in the treatment of schizophrenia. European Journal of Psychiatry, 5(1), 55–63.

Levitt J.J., McCarley R.W., Nestor P.G., Petrescu C., Donnino R., Hirayasu Y., Kikinis R., Jolesz F.A., & Shenton, M.E. (1999 July). Quantitative volumetric MRI study of the cerebellum and vermis in schizophrenia: Clinical and cognitive correlates. American Journal of Psychiatry, 156, 1105–1107.

Lindenmayer, J.P.: Berstein-Hyman, R.; Grochowski, S.; & Bark, N. (1995). Psychopathology of schizophrenia: initial validation of a 5-factor model. Psychopathology, 28, 22–31.

Littrell, K.H., Herth, K.A., & Hinte, L.E. (1996). The experience of hope in adults with schizophrenia. Psychiatric Rehabilitation Journal, 19(4), 61–65.

Luke A., Cooper, R., Prewitt, E., Adeyemo, A.A., & Forrester, T.E. (2001). Nutritional Consequences of the African Diaspora. Annual review of Nutrition, 21, 47–71.

Mattes, J.A. (1997). Risperidone: how good is the evidence for efficacy? Schizophrenia Bulletin, 23 (1), 155–161.

Martin, R. L. (1991, March). Outpatient management of schizophrenia. American Family Physician, 43(3), 921–933.

McCreadie, R., Macdonald, E., Blacklock, C., & Tilak-Singh, D. (1998, September). Dietary intake of schizophrenic patients in Nithsdale, Scotland: case control study. British Medical Journal, 317(7161), 784–785.

Meise, U., & Fleischacker, W. 1996. Perspectives on treatment needs in schizophrenia. British Journal of Psychiatry, 168(29), 9–16.

Mellor, J. E., Laugharne, D. E., & Peet, M. (1995). Schizophrenic Symptoms and Dietary Intake of n-3 Fatty Acids. Schizophrenia Research, 18, 85–86.

Mellor, J. E., Laugharne, D. E., & Peet, M. (1996). Omega-3 Fatty Acid Supplementation in Schizophrenic Patients. Human Psychopharmacology, 11, 39–46.

Menninger, Karl. (1963). The Vital Balance. New York: Viking Press.

Mosak, H.H. (1995). Drugless psychotherapy with schizophrenics. Individual Psychology. Journal of Adlerian Theory, Research, and Practice, 51 (1), 61–66.

Mukherjee, S. & Mahadik, S. P. (1994). A New Paradigm for Schizophrenia? Schizophrenia Research, 13, 191–194.

Mueser, K. T. (1996). Helping Families Manage Severe Mental Illness. Psychiatric Rehabilitation Skills, 1(2), 21–42.

Nigal, D., Calev, A., Kugelmass, S., & Lerer, B. (1991). Effect of four-week neuroleptic and anticholinergic drug withdrawal on memory function in chronic long-hospitalized schizophrenics. Annals of Clinical Psychiatry, 3(2), 141–145.

Omega-3 Mental Health Research Group. (2001). Diet and schizophrenia. Sheffield University. Retrieved July 10, 2001 from the World Wide Web <http://www.shef.ac.uk/uni/projects/omega3/dietand.htm>.

Ofuji, M., Kaiya, H., Nosaki, M., & Tsurumi, K. (1989). Platelet Prostaglandin E_1 Hyposensitivity in Schizophrenia: Reduction of Prostaglandin E_1- or Forskolin-Stimulated Cyclic AMP Response in Platelets. Life Sciences, 45, 2135–2140.

Rhoades, D. (2000). Schizophrenia: A Review for Family Counselors. Family Journal, 8, 258–267.

Rogers, P. & McNeil, I. (1996). "A Sense Of Purpose Inspired By A Sister's Schizophrenia." People, July 15, 1–3.

Rosberg, J. (2001). Some Notes on Schizophrenia and the Strategic Psychotherapy of Direct Confrontation. APS Newsletter. Retrieved on the World Wide Web 30 Nov. 2001, **http://www.schizophrenia-help.com/feb99.htm.**

Ross, M.F. (1999). University of Florida researchers cite possible link between autism, schizophrenia and diet. Science Daily. Retrieved July 10, 2001 from the World Wide Web **<http://www.sciencedaily.com/releases/1999/03/990316103010.htm>.**

Ruiz, P. (1965). The minority patient. Community Mental Health Journal, 21(3), 206–216.

Russell, A.J.; Munro, J.C.; Jones, P.B., et al. (1997). Schizophrenia and the myth of intellectual decline. American Journal Psychiatry, 154 (5), 635–639

Sartorius, N.; Gulbinat, W.; Harrison, G.; Laska, E.; & Siegel, C. (1996). Long-term follow-up of schizophrenia in 16 countries. Social Psychiatry & Psychiatric Epidemiology, 31, 249–258.

Schaub, A., Andres, K., Brenner, H.D., & Donzel, G. (1997). Developing a group format coping-oriented treatment program for schizophrenic patients. In H.D. Brenner, W. Boker, and R. Genner, Eds., Towards a Comprehensive Therapy for Schizophrenia. Gottingen, Germany: Hogrefe & Huber, 228–251.

Scheff, T. J. (1966). Being Mentally Ill: A Sociological Theory. Chicago: Aldine Publishing Company.

Schwartzberg, S., Wheelis, J., & Zarate, C.A. 1996. The danger of hopefulness: A clozapine "cure" of chronic psychosis. Harvard Review of Psychiatry, 4(3), 146–152.

"Schizophrenia." (2001). Healthwell. Retrieved July 10, 2001 from the World Wide Web at: **<http://www.healthwell. com/healthnotes/Concern/Schizophrenia.cfm>.**

Shenton M.E., Wible C.G., McCarley R.W. (1997). A review of magnetic resonance imaging studies of brain abnormalities in schizophrenia. In: K.P.R. Krishnan, & P.M. Doraiswamy (Eds.), Brain Imaging in Clinical Psychiatry. New York: Marcel Dekker, Inc.

Smith, T.E.; Shea, M.T.; Schooler, N.R.; Levin, H.; Deutsch, A.; & Grabstein, E. (1995). Studies of schizophrenia: personality traits in schizophrenia. Psychiatry, 58 (May), 99–113.

Smith, T.E.; Shea, M.T.; Schooler, N.R.; Levin, H.; Deutsch, A.; & Grabstein, E. (1995). Studies of schizophrenia: personality traits in schizophrenia. Psychiatry, 58 (May), 99–113.

Sullivan, H. S. (1953). Interpretation of Schizophrenia. New York: Norton.

Talan, J. (1997). "Path To Treatment." Newsday, Oct. 31, 1–3.

Tarrier, N. (1991a). Some aspects of family interventions in schizophrenia: I. Adherence to intervention programmes. British Journal of Psychiatry, 159, 475–480.

Tarrier, N. (1991b). Some aspects of family interventions in schizophrenia: II. Financial considerations. British Journal of Psychiatry, 159, 481–484.

Thase, M. E., Reynolds, C. F., Frank, E., & Simons, A. D. (1994, April). Do depressed men and women respond similarly to cognitive behavior? American Journal of Psychiatry, 151(4), 500–505.

Tollefson, G.D. (1996). Cognitive function in schizophrenic patients. Journal of Clinical Psychiatry, 57(11), 31–39.

Tien, A.Y.; Eaton, W.W.; Schlaepfer, T.E., et al. (1996). Exploratory factor analysis of MRI brain structure measures in schizophrenia. Schizophrenia Research, 19, 93–101.

Trierweiler, S.J., Thompson, E.E., Munday, C., Binion, V.J., & Gomez, J.P. (2000). Clinician attributions associated with the diagnosis of schizophrenia in African American and non-African American patients. Journal of Counseling and Clinical Psychology, 68(1), 171–175.

Vaddadi, K. S. (1991). Use of Gamma-Linolenic Acid in the Treatment of Schizophrenia and Tardive Dyskinesia. Prostaglandins Leukotrienes and Essential Fatty acids, 46, 67–70.

Vaddadi, K. S., Gilleard, C. J., Soosai, E., Polonowita, A. K., Gibson, R. A., & Burrows, G. D. (1996). Schizophrenia, Tardive Dyskinesia and Essential Fatty Acids. Schizophrenia Research, 20, 287–294.

Vallada, H.P. & Kunugi, H. (1996). A overview of schizophrenia genetic research presented at 1995 World Congress on Psychiatric Genetics, Cardiff. Schizophrenia Research, 19, 87–92.

Wahlberg, K.E.; Wynne, L.C.; Oja, H., et al. (1997). Gene-environment interaction in vulnerability to schizophrenia: findings from the Finnish adoptive family study of schizophrenia. American Journal of Psychiatry, 154 (3), 355–361.

Whittam Smith, A. (1997). "The Point Is Not What Causes Schizophrenia, But How To Control." Independent, Oct. 21, 1–3.

Wible C.G., Shenton M.E., Fischer I.A., Allard J.E., Kikinis R., Jolesz F.A., Iosifescu D.V., & McCarley R.W. (1997). Parcellation of the human prefrontal cortex using MRI. Psychiatry Research: Neuroimaging, 76, 29–40.

Worthington, C. (1992). An examination of the factors influencing diagnosis and treatment of Black patients in the mental health system. Archives of Psychiatric Nursing,6(3), 195–204.

Wyatt, R.J.; Apud, J.A.; & Potkin, S. (1996). New directions in the prevention and treatment of schizophrenia: a biological perspective. Psychiatry, 59 (Winter), 357–369.
(1997). Schizophrenia: Public Information. American Psychiatric Association. Jan. 9, 1996, 1–15. "Schizophrenia." Microsoft Encarta. CD-ROM, 1.

Wyatt, R.J.; Apud, J.A.; & Potkin, S. (1996). New directions in the prevention and treatment of schizophrenia: a biological perspective. Psychiatry, 59 (Winter), 357–369.

Wyatt, R.J.; Apud, J.A.; & Potkin, S. (1996). New directions in the prevention and treatment of schizophrenia: a biological perspective, Psychiatry, 59 (Winter), 357–369.

Zane, N., Enomoto, K., & Chun, C.A. (1994). Treatment outcomes of Asian and white American clients. Journal of Community Psychology, 22 (2), 177–191.

Zhang, D. (1995). Depression and culture: The Chinese Perspective. Canadian Journal of Counseling, 29(3), 227–233.

0-595-25675-9